AMERICAN MURDER HOUSES

AMERICAN MURDER HOUSES

A Coast-to-Coast Tour of the Most
Notorious Houses of Homicide

STEVE LEHTO

BERKLEY BOOKS, NEW YORK

THE BERKLEY PUBLISHING GROUP
Published by the Penguin Group
Penguin Group (USA) LLC
375 Hudson Street, New York, New York 10014

USA • Canada • UK • Ireland • Australia • New Zealand • India • South Africa • China

penguin.com

A Penguin Random House Company

This book is an original publication of The Berkley Publishing Group.

Copyright © 2015 by Steve Lehto.

Library of Congress Cataloging-in-Publication Data

Lehto, Steve.
American murder houses : a coast-to-coast tour of the most notorious houses of homicide / Steve Lehto.
pages cm
ISBN 978-0-425-26251-1 (paperback)
1. Murder—United States—History.   2. Crime scenes—United States—History.   I. Title.
HV6524.L44 2015
364.152'30973—dc23
2014035749

PUBLISHING HISTORY
Berkley trade paperback edition / February 2015

PRINTED IN THE UNITED STATES OF AMERICA

10 9 8 7 6 5 4 3 2 1

Cover photo by Getty Images.
Cover design by George Long.
Interior text design by Laura K. Corless.

CONTENTS

CONTENTS

CONTENTS

CONTENTS

Foreword

On a sunny weekend in January 2013, I visited Miami Beach and had lunch with a friend at the News Café on Ocean Drive. I was in the process of finishing this book on American murder houses and knew that one such house was within walking distance of where we were sitting: the home that had been owned by Gianni Versace. In fact, Versace had walked from his home to the News Café on the morning of July 15, 1997, and it was on his return trip that he was gunned down on his front steps by a serial killer named Andrew Cunanan. After lunch, my friend and I walked up the street toward the mansion, the same path Versace took that fateful day. Versace's walk would have been a little easier; he was walking on a Tuesday morning when the foot traffic would have been a bit lighter than what we encountered.

Ocean Drive along this stretch of Miami Beach is a beautiful wall of Art Deco buildings facing the water, most of them restaurants and hotels. Tucked in among them is one home: the mansion where Versace lived. The day we walked by, the mansion was being operated as an upscale hotel and restaurant. I wondered if many people would know or remember that Versace was murdered there fifteen years ago?

As we approached the house we noticed people standing in front of the mansion's black iron gates, posing for pictures. A security guard stood just inside the gates, keeping an eye on the visitors and the front of the building. As one group of tourists would leave, another would wander by. Invariably, the passersby would look around, pose for pictures in front of the gates, and move on. Did all these people know about Versace and that he had died here? Apparently so. There were no signs on the spot and nothing to indicate who used to own the home or who might have died here. And still, there was a steady stream of visitors to the front steps, many getting their pictures taken in front of a pair of otherwise bland-looking metal gates.

This, a decade and a half after Gianni Versace's murder, was a testament to the attraction of the murder house. There is no question that Americans are fascinated with murder houses and always have been. After a murder hits the news, people are seemingly drawn to the scene of the crime. One of the most common postmurder images on the news is of the curious gathered in front of a house, sometimes holding a vigil in remembrance of the dead. Some may be there to comfort survivors, and sometimes friends and relatives comfort one another. Neighbors often join those who have traveled to come see the crime scene. Eventually, the number of people in front of the home will dwindle, but the murder house will always retain a certain stigma and attract attention long after the vigils end. Nowadays, websites are devoted to murder houses, with aficionados often checking in and telling of recent visits and observations.

But what makes anyone want to go and look at a murder house, after the police tape has been removed and the reporters have moved on to other stories? It is hard to say. Americans have a fascination with crime. True-crime programs on television are quite popular and there is always a certain amount of drama in any murder case. What would drive someone to kill another person? What if the accused didn't do it? Imagine the horror of being charged with a crime you didn't commit. What about the unsolved crimes? If the murderer is still out there, will he strike again? Each murder seems to raise questions like these and more. Once the crime scenes have been studied and the trials completed, all that remains for the curious is the murder house.

This book is a collection of twenty-nine well-known murder houses from around the country. They run the spectrum of time, from the 1830s to the twenty-first century. Some were home to famous people who were murdered; others were homes for regular, nonfamous people who only became famous for how they died. In some, the killers were much more famous before the murders than the victims. Not all the crimes were solved. For example, people still argue about whether Lizzie

Borden hacked her parents to death with a hatchet. Not all killers were brought to justice; many people have strong beliefs about who killed Nicole Brown Simpson and Ronald Goldman, but no one was ever convicted for their murders. The Los Angeles Police Department famously announced it had no intention of looking any further for their killer; to them, the case was solved.

Some of the murder houses have murkier histories. At least one famous murder house is on lists like these only because of a hoax. The legend surrounding the house was invented from thin air; we do not know who started it or why, but today people go and look at the house where no one was murdered—because they have heard that people were killed there in a most spectacular and gruesome manner. In that instance I explain what we do know about the home and where the story most likely sprang from. If I hadn't, it would have appeared to be a glaring omission to those who had heard of it but did not know it was a hoax.

Some murder houses became famous only because of books written about the murders that occurred in them. Truman Capote thrust the Clutter house of Holcomb, Kansas, into the public eye with his book *In Cold Blood*. The family that briefly lived in the DeFeo house in Amityville, New York, wrote a book—which they claimed was a true story—about their former home and how it was possessed by evil spirits. The evil spirits were not real, but the DeFeos, who had been murdered in the house before the Lutz family "fled" from the house, were all too real. The story of their murder house's alleged haunting has overshadowed the DeFeos' own sad end.

Many other murder houses have been demolished or are long gone. A few of them are mentioned in this book but are not featured. Some probably would have been knocked down regardless of their history, but others most certainly were leveled to erase the stigma of the home's past. The Hale-Bopp "Heaven's Gate" house is one example. The Sharon Tate murder house was razed decades after the Manson Family killed its occupants, and the home owned by John Wayne Gacy has long since been replaced with another home on the same lot where Gacy buried many of his victims. More than a few famous murder houses have burned down, some under mysterious circumstances. That of Ed Gein, for instance, burned down not long after he was arrested. Arson was suspected, and considering the gruesomeness of his crimes—he killed and gutted one victim, and also admitted digging up and stealing bodies from the local cemetery—no one in the community bothered to find out who did it.

As of this writing, the homes described here are still standing. The following accounts and descriptions of the most well-known American murder houses and the murders that put them on this list are as factual as possible. Each chapter is followed by a reference or two indicating a good starting place for a reader who wants to see more information on a given murder house.

Keep in mind that most of these houses are owned by private individuals who are not seeking any particular attention. Still, many of these houses can be seen without intruding onto the property. If you choose to go look at any of them, you should be careful to remain on public property. The few houses that are open for tours are noted, and, of course, you can inspect those houses to your heart's content. Included here are the addresses and many other details of the houses, all available from public sources with a little bit of digging. These cases were well publicized and the information is public and out there for anyone to obtain. Even so, please respect the privacy of the owners. Their homes have been through a lot.

Lady Nero Tortures Her Slaves

THE LALAURIE MANSION

1834

1140 Royal Street
New Orleans, Louisiana 70116

On April 10, 1834, smoke poured from the LaLaurie mansion, a huge home in the French Quarter of New Orleans owned by socialite Delphine LaLaurie and her wealthy husband, Dr. Louis LaLaurie. The fire had started in the kitchen and spread quickly through the house. As flames engulfed the two-story structure, the LaLauries ran into the street and implored neighbors to help them retrieve their furniture and antiques from the inferno. As volunteers rushed forward, someone in the crowd stepped up and asked: Aren't there still people in the house as well?

There were. It would be a few decades before slavery was abolished, and the LaLauries owned slaves. They called them "servants" and the community knew all too well about them. Delphine had even been brought to court, charged with abusing her slaves, and now it was only natural to wonder where they were as the house burned. They were not outside. Why weren't the LaLauries in a hurry to rescue them along with their other belongings? It seemed very odd. If nothing else, the slaves could be helping to empty the house. The LaLauries were hiding something. Louis responded to the neighbor by saying, "Never mind the servants, save my valuables." For reasons no one can fully explain, that comment would later be attributed to his wife, Delphine. And slaves were valuable. Why wouldn't they want to save them?

People in the crowd became enraged when they realized there were servants in the house whom the LaLauries were willing to let burn to death. Many had heard about Delphine's earlier court case, but rumors had traveled through the neighborhood that the LaLauries kept their slaves chained in cramped quarters within the house. Some men ran into the house specifically to find the slaves the LaLauries had condemned to death. Kicking down locked doors, they barged into the slave quarters. There, they found slaves chained to the floor, with iron shackles around their necks and ankles. The local *New Orleans Bee* newspaper reported, "Seven slaves more or less horribly mutilated were seen suspended by the neck, with their limbs apparently stretched and torn from one extremity to the other. Language is powerless and inadequate to give a proper conception of the horror which a scene like this must have inspired." The paper reported the slaves were not just being mistreated—they were clearly being tortured. Some were in such bad condition that rescuers feared they might die from the injuries they suffered before they had been rescued from the fire. The townspeople were convinced that Delphine was the guilty party and that her husband, the doctor, had little responsibility for the crimes. Again, we do not know why this was the consensus at the time. The rescuers removed the slaves from the home and took them for medical treatment and then to the police station. Authorities were trying to determine what steps they should take next. The cause of the fire was never determined, but many people said it had been started by an abused slave to spite her cruel master, Delphine LaLaurie.

Medical personnel were shocked by what they saw when treating the LaLaurie slaves. Some of the slaves bore festering wounds infested with maggots; others had obvious signs of intentional injuries inflicted upon them, such as drill holes in their skulls. At least one slave could not walk because of severely injured legs. The scandal mushroomed as word spread through the community of the bizarre and cruel injuries the slaves had suffered before the fire destroyed much of the LaLaurie mansion. The *New Orleans Bee* reported that thousands of people came by the police station to view the slaves, having heard of the atrocities and wanting to see if the story was true. The paper then reported that many of the angry citizens made their way to the LaLaurie mansion, where they "demolished and destroyed everything upon which they could lay their hands. . . . the mob remained still unabated and threatens the total demolition of the entire edifice." The police were called to restore order. The house was not destroyed by the angry mob, but the paper reported that much of what the LaLauries had saved from the fire was.

The mob was not content to just smash the LaLauries' furniture. Calls went up for Delphine to come out and answer for her actions. Realizing there was no way she could remain in her home, and fearing the crowd outside might turn into a lynch mob, she hitched up a carriage and she and her husband raced away from the city, escaping some who tried pursuing them. They were rumored to have fled to the docks, where they had paid a handsome amount in gold to a ship's captain to take them immediately to either New York City or Paris. From there, the LaLauries faded from history. Stories persisted that they lived in exile in Paris, and that possibly, in her old age, Delphine had returned to the city in secret, where she finally died with no one taking notice. The house remained as a gruesome reminder that even in the homes of the rich, unspeakable things might be happening behind closed doors.

Despite its lurid reputation, the house was eventually sold to others and repaired. The tales of torture and murder would follow the home from owner to owner through the decades.

From time to time the story would reappear in local papers, discussing the history of the house and its former owners. They had dubbed Delphine "Lady Nero," and the LaLaurie mansion became renowned as a house of horrors. The legend of the house grew over time and, as so often happens, the story was embellished and exaggerated, becoming more horrific with each telling. Dozens of people were said to have been killed in the house, making Delphine one of the most reviled characters in Louisiana history. She was said to have hidden corpses in a well on the property and to have buried murder victims in her courtyard.

The LaLaurie mansion still stands in the French Quarter, but how much of Lady Nero's story is true? Delphine's marriage to Dr. Louis LaLaurie was her third, but the French doctor, who was twenty years her junior, provided a lifestyle unlike any she had been able to afford previously. The house they purchased on Royal Street in 1831 was palatial—although it was only two stories tall then—and Delphine would soon become known for her extravagant parties, to which she invited the better elements of New Orleans society. At the time, New Orleans was the fifth-largest city in the United States, with a population of more than forty-six thousand. To maintain the residence and throw the huge parties, Delphine kept several servants—slaves—in the house.

During this time, neighbors whispered that Delphine treated her slaves cruelly. Although slavery was legal at the time, slave owners were still expected to treat their slaves with some modicum of humanity. Delphine apparently didn't think such notions applied to her. Within just a few years of moving into the home, Delphine was brought to court, accused of physically abusing one of her slaves. The charges were not criminal in nature; abuse of a slave was considered only a civil matter at the time. That is, one could be fined for the infraction but not put in jail. As a result, her criminal record remained untarnished. We do not know if Delphine was found liable and paid a fine, or if the charges were dismissed. Either way, that was the last anyone heard of her poorly treated slaves until the day of the fire. And the story of the slaves being saved from the burning house was also true. It is at that point where the story shifts from history into myth.

When the LaLauries left New Orleans, the legend of what happened in their house began to grow. Nowadays, embellished and exaggerated stories of the LaLaurie mansion are easy to find. Instead of slaves being tortured, most stories claim slaves were murdered in the home. According to some accounts, as many as fifty or sixty slaves were murdered at the LaLaurie mansion. Most stories include among the victims a young slave girl who fell or was pushed from the roof by Delphine; others tell of dozens of slaves killed and buried on the property. Notwithstanding the stories, there is no evidence that a slave girl ever died from a fall on the premises. Further, there were no murdered slaves or buried victims on the premises. The story of the fire in 1834 was well publicized, but none of the contemporaneous reports mention anyone dying or being murdered in the house before the fire. Further, when the slaves were found at the house during the fire, none of them were dead. It is true that the seven who were rescued were in rough shape and some of them may have died later from their pre-fire injuries, but no one can unearth any documentation of any charges ever levied against the LaLauries resulting from the discovery of the slaves in the burning house. It appears that most of the stories about the LaLauries sprang from the initial reports of cruelty to the slaves at the house and the one time Delphine was brought to court for mistreating a slave. Without question, the LaLauries tortured their slaves and treated them worse than animals; they certainly valued their furniture more than the slaves' lives. But no one was murdered in the house. Be that as it may, countless people flock to the mansion today, to see the home where the cruel Mrs. LaLaurie tortured and killed her slaves.

And how does one disprove the stories of the countless murders and the bodies buried secretly on the premises? It takes little evidence to start a legend. Disproving one is a different problem altogether. More than a hundred years later, researchers would reconstruct the events at the LaLaurie mansion and Delphine's movements after the fire. Much of the legend of the LaLauries had simply been embellished to add drama to the tale, like a good ghost story. It is true that Delphine fled New Orleans; she went to Mobile, Alabama. From there, she traveled to New York City and then to Paris, where she lived openly for several years. There is no indication that anyone pursued her to Europe or that authorities chased after her.

Most surprisingly, she then returned to New Orleans. The mansion she had lived in with her husband had long since been repaired and changed hands. Delphine settled in a different neighborhood in New Orleans, and her husband was no longer with her. It appeared that the LaLauries had gotten divorced and the doctor had started a new life in Cuba. Delphine's name appeared in a city directory in 1850, and a legal action was also filed in her name that year. She was not, however, in the directory in 1852, and her estate was settled in 1856, indicating that she had probably died in the early 1850s. Still, there was no record of her encountering any legal problems in her later life, which might have resulted if she had really been suspected or accused of killing slaves at her mansion before her move to Europe. And, of course, if she had been suspected of murder, she could have been charged when she returned to New Orleans. She never was charged and there was no indication that she ever took any steps to hide from public view.

The LaLaurie mansion, built in 1832, stands at 1140 Royal Street, three stories tall now, with a wrought-iron balcony on the second floor and distinctive arched windows on all floors. The third story was added to it in 1850, right around the time that Delphine died. The 10,248 square foot home is considered to be in the French Empire style. It has six bedrooms, and two and a half bathrooms, and—as with many "murder" houses—is said by many to be haunted. The tall structure wraps around a courtyard that is now paved with bricks. Stalwart believers in the murdered-slaves theory would suggest there are bodies of murder victims beneath the courtyard.

The house was used for a variety of purposes over the years after the LaLauries moved out. In fact, the uses to which it was put were quite wide-ranging. It became a public school, a music conservatory, a bar, and then a furniture store. By 1937, the home at 1140 Royal Street was more commonly known as the Warrington House, named for a more recent owner. Even so, postcards depicting the house suggested it was haunted and mention the cruel Delphine. The Historic American Buildings Survey contains a photograph of the house, taken in 1937, captioned *1140 Royal Street, Haunted House (Warrington House)*.

In April 2007, it was widely reported that actor Nicolas Cage had purchased the home for $3.45 million, one of many historic homes around the country that Cage had purchased—including another one in New Orleans. Only two years after buying it, Cage placed the LaLaurie mansion back on the market with an asking price of $3.9 million. Although the price was later reduced to $3.55 million, a buyer failed to materialize, and in 2009 a bank foreclosed on the property. It was listed for sale in 2010 with an asking price of $2.9 million, but again there were no buyers. The listing was quietly removed that August.

The home sits prominently on the corner of Royal Street and Governor Nicholls Street. Just two blocks down Governor Nicholls Street is another mansion from the 1830s owned by famous people. Angelina Jolie and Brad Pitt bought the home at 521 Governor Nicholls Street for a reported $3.5 million.

Today, many visitors to New Orleans make a special trip to see the home where Delphine was said to have tortured and killed her slaves in a most barbaric fashion. The true facts of the case matter little to many of the visitors; the story is more interesting the way it is commonly told. The LaLaurie mansion is easy to find and the exterior is visible from the street, but keep in mind that it is privately owned. Whether you choose to believe the stories of hauntings and murders in the LaLaurie mansion is entirely up to you.

* Victoria Cosner Love and Lorelei Shannon, *Mad Madame LaLaurie: New Orleans's Most Famous Murderess Revealed* (2011).

The Infamous Axe Murders—
But Did She Kill Her Parents?

THE LIZZIE BORDEN HOUSE

1892

230 Second Street (formerly 92 Second Street)
Fall River, Massachusetts 02721

On a pleasant Thursday morning in Fall River, Massachusetts, August 4, 1892, Abby and Andrew Borden were at home with their adult daughter and their maid. Abby was sixty-four years old, taking a nap in an upstairs room of their home, while Andrew, who would have turned seventy in September, relaxed in a downstairs parlor. Their thirty-two-year-old daughter, Lizzie, had chores of her own to attend to, and the neighborhood was quiet. Around eleven o'clock in the morning, someone quietly entered the room where Abby was napping and struck her in the head with a hatchet, killing her almost instantly. The attacker struck her in the head again and again, nineteen times in all, brutally disfiguring her face.

Yet no one else in the house heard a thing. The ferocity of the attack would stun investigators.

The killer then remained in the house—hidden, since there were others in the house—for more than an hour and struck again. This time, Andrew was bludgeoned in a downstairs sitting room. Using the same hatchet or axe as before, the killer hit Andrew in the face and head eleven times, leaving his body sprawled on the couch, covered in blood and badly mangled. The two victims were each hacked and beaten far more than was necessary to kill them. Investigators would later conclude that the murderer must have been filled with rage.

The murders would be discovered when Lizzie walked into the downstairs parlor and found her father's bloody body. She became hysterical and began screaming for help. The maid rushed downstairs from her third-floor room. Soon, the house was abuzz with neighbors and police. Someone went upstairs to break the news to Abby—everyone had assumed she was upstairs napping—and found her hacked to death in the guest bedroom. Investigators noticed that the blood near Abby had dried and her body was much colder to the touch than Andrew's had been. They realized that the two murders had occurred an hour or more apart. Adding to the mystery, both had been killed in broad daylight, while Lizzie and the maid were in the house.

The case of Lizzie Borden—for she would be the one accused of killing her parents—would become one of America's most well-known crimes. As a result, Lizzie Borden would attain legendary status as an accused murderer, a fact underscored by her name recognition today. The murders were seemingly known by everyone in nineteenth-century America and were even immortalized in a children's nursery rhyme that many people know today, over a hundred years later:

> *Lizzie Borden took an axe*
> *And gave her mother forty whacks.*
> *When she saw what she had done*
> *She gave her father forty-one.*

The numbers in the nursery rhyme are inaccurate and Lizzie was never convicted of the murders, so perhaps it also names the wrong person wielding the axe. Still, the popularity of the ditty shows how widely known the crime was: At the time, the murder was sensationalized by newspapers across the country and gained a national audience. This was unusual at the time since the Bordens were not known outside their town; normally, a criminal trial like this would only make local newspapers. The gruesomeness of the crime, and the allegation that the axe-wielding murderer was a single woman, added fuel to the fire.

Headlines screamed of the "Shocking Crime" and vividly described how the victims were "hacked to pieces in their own home." People studying crime history in America are often amazed at how news coverage of murders has changed over the years. The Lizzie Borden case is a great example of how gory the news coverage was in the old days. Regardless of who committed the murders, they happened in a house that still stands today and is being operated as a bed-and-breakfast. Students of murder mysteries can visit the home, examine the crime scenes, and even spend the night.

Lizzie Andrew Borden was born in 1860, and her mother died when she was two and a half years old. Her father, Andrew Jackson Borden, remarried. Abby Durfee Borden became Lizzie's stepmother, but Lizzie and Abby did not always get along well. Somewhere during the next quarter century, Lizzie began calling her stepmother "Mrs. Borden," rather than the more familiar "Mother." The Bordens were well-to-do; Andrew headed a local bank and in today's dollars would have been a multimillionaire. At age thirty-two Lizzie still lived at home, which was a simple two-story structure with an attic that had been built in the 1840s. Fall River was by no means a small town, with seventy-five thousand inhabitants. Soon, they would all know about Lizzie Borden.

A search of the house after the murders turned up the head of a hatchet in the basement of the house but no other evidence of a murder weapon. In fact, the hatchet's handle was never found and there was no blood on the hatchet, leading some to believe that it was not the murder weapon. No other likely weapon was ever located. There were other oddities about the crime scenes. Surprisingly little blood was found anywhere except on the bodies of the victims. Shouldn't there have been blood on the furniture, the floor, or the attacker? Could a killer have moved from room to room in the house without leaving some kind of bloody trail? And there were only two other people in the house at the time of the killings: Lizzie and the maid, Bridget Sullivan. And no one suspected the maid. Both claimed to have heard nothing out of the ordinary during the time frame within which the killings occurred.

Various rumors circulated about who might want to harm the Bordens, but attention soon focused on Lizzie. She had been in the house at the time of the murders and her story seemed inconsistent. Parts of it also seemed implausible. How could she have been in the house during the murders and not have heard anything? Neighbors heard nothing unusual in or around the house, and no one was seen entering or leaving the house. Lizzie also told some contradictory stories that seemed to be fabrications, leading some to believe she was concocting alibis rather than telling the truth about what happened that day.

A two-day inquest was begun on August 9, five days after the murders, and Lizzie was grilled by the local prosecutor for four hours in front of a magistrate. She was not represented by counsel. She denied any knowledge of who killed her parents but freely admitted her troubled relationship with her stepmother. She knew of no one who might want to harm her family. She had not heard anything unusual in the house when her parents were being hacked to death. She said that when she looked into the room where her father was killed, she saw the blood and ran out to call for help. The prosecutor found it hard to believe when she claimed to not realize that her father was dead the moment she first saw him. He displayed little tact as he cross-examined her:

Lizzie: "I opened the door and rushed back."

Q: "[You] looked in at the door?"

A: "I opened the door and rushed back."

Q: "[You] saw his face?"

A: "No, I did not see his face because he was all covered with blood."

Q: "Did you see his eye-ball hanging out?"

A: "No, sir."

Q: "See the gashes where his face was laid open?"

A: "No, sir."

Finding her story unbelievable, the prosecutor insisted she be arrested for the murders. On August 11, Lizzie was arrested and the press went wild. Soon, newspapers across America were covering their front pages with the story. Many of the accounts were filled with the most gruesome details of the killings and speculation and rumors about motives and possible alternative suspects.

The legal process called for Lizzie to be arraigned and then face a grand jury, which would also call other witnesses and decide if there was enough evidence to put her on trial. After conducting its own investigation, the grand jury dithered. Not enough members believed there was enough evidence pointing to Lizzie as the killer. The grand jury was called back into session and the prosecution presented one more witness: A friend of Lizzie's would testify that she saw Lizzie burn a dress a few days after the killings. When asked, Lizzie had reportedly said that she had gotten paint on the dress. That was apparently enough for the grand jury to change its mind and return an indictment. Lizzie would face trial for the axe murder of her father and stepmother.

In 1893, the Lizzie Borden trial captivated the nation. The proceedings were held before a panel of three judges, and the prosecution pulled out all the stops in presenting its case. Two prosecutors handled the case. Lizzie hired two lawyers, one of whom, George Robinson, had been the governor of Massachusetts just six years earlier. Robinson was a Harvard graduate who had spent more than a dozen years in various political offices. He reportedly charged Lizzie $25,000 for his services, but the money would be well spent.

The trial provided more than enough drama to remain front-page news across the country. The prosecution brought Andrew and Abby Borden's skulls to the courtroom, intending to show them to the jury and introduce them into evidence. During the opening statements, one of the attorneys accidentally knocked Andrew's skull, which had been covered, so that it dramatically appeared uncovered in front of Lizzie. In typical fashion for a lady of her era, she fainted at the sight of it and the trial was delayed for a few moments until the skull was covered and she regained her composure. It later came out in testimony that the doctor who had performed the autopsies on the victims had not sought permission from the Borden daughters to remove the heads of the victims and had not even told them about it before the trial began. He had simply cut off their heads, reduced them to skulls, and brought them to court as he would any other trial exhibits.

More surprises came during trial testimony. A doctor from Harvard Medical School testified that he had examined the stomach contents of the victims—they had been removed at the same time as the heads—and found no evidence of poison. The theory that the family had been poisoned had gained some traction because all of its members—Lizzie, her sister, and the parents—had all been ill in the days before the murders. While the pronouncement that there was no poison in the victims' stomachs might not have seemed all that remarkable, what the doctor said next was. He was certain that Mrs. Borden had been killed *an hour and a half* before Mr. Borden had been murdered. Presumably, this meant that the killer had remained in the house for an hour and a half after killing Mrs. Borden, waiting for the opportunity to kill Mr. Borden.

If it had been Lizzie, how come no one noticed her acting oddly during that time? Could she really have been so calculating that she could act normally so soon after hacking her stepmother to death? On the other hand, could a stranger have successfully waited in hiding inside the house for ninety minutes between the killings without being detected by Lizzie or the maid? The pieces of the puzzle did not appear to be able to fit no matter how much the prosecution manipulated them.

Journalists across the nation reported updates from the murder trial, and hungry readers speculated: What did the murderer do in that hour and a half? Other theories were floated: Was the murderer a disgruntled "Portugese" worker who had exchanged harsh words with Mr. Borden earlier in the day? If so, it wouldn't be much of a lead; the town was known to have a large Portuguese-American community, largely composed of men working in the whaling and fishing trade. Others wondered: Could the thirty-two-year-old unmarried daughter who still lived at home with her parents really be the one who hacked them to death? What would her motive have been?

The prosecution also had to answer several questions raised by the lack of physical evidence. How could Lizzie have so brutally killed two people without getting blood all over herself? The prosecutors floated a bizarre theory: Lizzie may have committed the murders while naked. This raised more questions—even as it generated murmurs from newspaper readers—about how she could have been running around her house naked for a couple hours without anyone else noticing. After all, the murders were committed during daylight hours and the maid was home the entire time.

While many members of the public may have been ready to convict Lizzie based on what they heard, the trial judges kept some of the more damning evidence from the jury. The jury did not hear that Lizzie had tried buying poison shortly before the killings. Better for Lizzie, her attorneys had successfully argued that her inquest testimony—where she had testified without an attorney—should be suppressed because she had not been advised of her rights before questioning. As a result, the jury did not get to hear any of Lizzie's lengthy inquest testimony where she had given confused and contradictory answers to some of the questions she had been asked. A good prosecutor could have used the testimony to show how Lizzie's story had not remained consistent. Since Lizzie did not testify at her murder trial, and the inquest testimony was kept from them, the jury never got to hear most of Lizzie's version of what had happened that day. The jury did hear from Lizzie's older sister, Emma, who told the court that Lizzie's relationship with her parents was unremarkable— certainly not of the sort that might lead to murder.

Even so, the testimony fueled arguments for both sides. When a doctor testified that he had been called to the house the day of the killings, Lizzie had told him an alibi that later seemed questionable. She had told him that she had been in the barn behind the house, looking for sinkers—lead weights for fishing—around the time of the murders and perhaps that was why she hadn't heard anything. But investigators had searched the barn when they had been summoned to the house, and they had found no indication that anyone had been in the barn that day. The floor was covered in dust and showed no footprints. The doctor also admitted, though, that he had prescribed morphine to Lizzie that day to calm her down. Perhaps that had caused her to give muddled and confused answers to investigators. Lizzie's attorneys seemed able to discredit almost every witness the prosecution produced, with newspapers suggesting that many of the prosecution witnesses ended up helping Lizzie's case by the time they left the stand.

It took the jury only an hour and a half to deliberate. They found Lizzie not guilty. Although many people today believe Lizzie killed her parents, the press that had breathlessly covered the trial appeared to support the verdict. The *New York Times* spoke favorably of the verdict and wrote scathing remarks about the inept members of law enforcement who had arrested and prosecuted the wrong person for the murders. Even so, many people in the community believed that Lizzie must have been involved on some level, and she found herself shunned by the Fall River community. Interestingly, the two daughters had inherited the estate because of the order in which Mr. and Mrs. Borden were murdered. Since the stepmother died first, the court ruled that her estate passed to her husband—if even for just an hour and a half—and became part of his estate, which then passed to his two daughters when he died. If the order of the deaths had been reversed, Lizzie and Emma might have received nothing, with everything in both estates passing to their stepmother's other relatives.

Lizzie and her sister bought another house nearby and moved out of the murder house. Their new home was huge and only a mile from the murder house. Located at 306 French Street in Fall River, it had eight bedrooms and three bedrooms. Known as "Maplecroft," it was almost four thousand square feet. It was also newer than their old house, having been built in 1900. It was built in the Queen Anne style and it still stands. In fact, it was in the news recently when its current owner placed it on the market in 2012, asking $650,000 for it.

The Borden sisters lived together for a while, but they eventually had a falling-out. Lizzie died in 1927 and was buried at the Oak Grove Cemetery, about a mile and half from the home where here parents were murdered. She was sixty-seven years old. She was buried in the family plot. Nearby are the graves of her parents and her sister.

Fall River is an hour south of Boston and less than half an hour east of Providence, Rhode Island. The city's two attractions are the Lizzie Borden house and Battleship Cove, a park and museum where visitors can inspect the decommissioned USS *Massachusetts* along with a retired destroyer and a World War II submarine. What soon became known as the Lizzie Borden House was a private residence until 1986. Then, the current owners decided to open it up as the Lizzie Borden Bed & Breakfast Museum. Overnight guests are welcome to stay in one of the six bedrooms; as many as eighteen guests can be accommodated. The house is also open for tours, which take visitors through the home in a one-and-a-half to two-hour trip back to the time of the murders. The home has been expertly restored to as close to the original condition as possible. Time does not permit for most tours to visit the basement, although it is included in the evening tours that are given to overnight guests. The basement is where the hatchet—which the prosecution believed was the murder weapon—was found.

A barn has been reconstructed out back to resemble the one Lizzie talked about being in while doing some errands the day of the murders. The original barn had burned down in 1929 and its replacement now houses the museum, where the bestselling item is a Lizzie Borden bobblehead doll, for $20.

Some people are convinced the house is haunted. Students of the paranormal often visit and describe seeing and feeling things that evidence the spirits of Andrew and Abby still residing within the house. Regardless of what you believe or who you believe committed the murders, you are welcome to visit the Lizzie Borden Bed & Breakfast Museum—as tens of thousands do each year—and investigate for yourself.

---

* Lizzie Borden Bed & Breakfast Museum ("Where Everyone Is Treated Like Family"), lizzie-borden.com.

"Cosmos Mariner—
Destination Unknown"

THE CONRAD AIKEN HOUSE

1901

228 East Oglethorpe Avenue
Savannah, Georgia 31401

On the night of February 26, 1901, an eleven-year-old boy named Conrad Aiken heard his parents fighting, long into the night and the next morning. The family lived in Savannah, Georgia, where the father had a medical practice. Dr. Aiken suffered from mental illness and often fought with Conrad's mother. The young boy had become accustomed to his father's outbursts and thought little of this fight at first. This night, his father was hurling accusations at his mother; her replies were ignored by the doctor. She had long since learned to weather these fights by simply letting her husband rant and rave until he ran out of steam, and Conrad had likewise learned to simply ignore the yelling until it stopped. Then

Conrad heard his father shouting, "One, two three!" followed by the sound of a gunshot. A moment later, a second "One, two three!" was followed by another gunshot, and then Conrad heard the thud of his father's body crumpling to the floor. Dr. Aiken had fatally shot Conrad's mother and then himself. The local newspapermen described it a bit more graphically, saying that after he shot his wife, Dr. Aiken had "sent a bullet crashing through his own brain." Conrad was the oldest of four children at home at the time of the killings.

Conrad went into his parents' bedroom and discovered their bodies. He went downstairs and told the servants what had happened and asked them to attend to his three siblings while he reported the shootings to the police. He then ran barefoot to the nearby police station, where he told them, "Papa has shot Momma." Local authorities went to the house but didn't do too much investigation, as it was pretty obvious what had happened.

Although little known today, Conrad Aiken would grow up to be a well-renowned poet in his day, winner of a Pulitzer Prize and many other accolades for his writing. The Savannah house Conrad Aiken grew up in would become famous for what happened in it when Conrad was eleven years old.

Conrad Potter Aiken was born August 5, 1889, the child of a physician and his wife, William Ford Aiken and Anna Aiken. Dr. Aiken was both an "oculist" and an "aurist" according to local papers, which meant that he treated problems of both vision and hearing. He graduated from Harvard Medical

School in 1886 but also dabbled in other pursuits such as invention and photography. The family lived in Savannah, Georgia, and Conrad's childhood was pleasant and unremarkable at first. He idolized his father; at one point he was asked by an adult what he thought God looked like, and he replied, "God must be very like my father when he smiled." As time went on, his father smiled less and argued often with Conrad's mother. Conrad also adored his mother, learning to read as he followed along in books she read to him. He jokingly told people later that as a result, he had learned to read "upside down." Although he had learned to read young and would later become a famous writer, he did not start school until he was ten or so. He later attributed it to parental neglect. He said, "My parents lost track of me. . . . I just ran wild."

The Aikens had moved to a bigger home as the family expanded, and Conrad reached eleven years of age while living in one of four units in a brick building called Marshall's Row on East Oglethorpe Avenue in Savannah. The Greek Revival building was three stories tall, and each unit had its own front and back door on the second level. Dr. Aiken used the lower level as his office where he met and treated patients. The family's servants lived in quarters behind the doctor's office, also on the lower floor. The bottom level had its own entrances to the street.

Conrad's life in the big home was marked by fights between his parents. Later, Conrad would write that the arguments his parents had were part of the fabric of his young life. Many of the arguments would focus on the mundane, like money problems, but would be fueled by bizarre behavior on the part of his father. He would often change the topic of the arguments and throw crazy accusations at his wife. The physician had attempted suicide a couple of times and may have been suffering from an untreated mental illness. Once, he took an overdose of drugs and left a note as to how he wanted his burial handled. Anna found him and called for medical help, and another doctor who lived nearby managed to revive him. On the second occasion he turned the gas on in the master bedroom, but Anna spotted the open valve and shut it off before anyone was hurt.

After the murder-suicide of his parents, local papers carried notices of his parents' deaths. "Dr. Aiken was wealthy and had a very large practice. Of late, however, he has been nervous and irritable. His friends attribute the tragedy to dementia from overwork and study. He was a deep student and often worked all night in his office at scientific investigation." Another paper ran a rather abbreviated death notice: "At Savannah, Ga, Dr. William F. Aiken killed his wife and self. Unsound mentally." If this was an unfitting obituary for the couple, their son Conrad would remedy that with a lifetime of writing, haunted by the deaths. Conrad went to live with relatives in Massachusetts.

Conrad thrived in Massachusetts and later attended Harvard, where his literary talents blossomed. He wrote for the Harvard publication *The Advocate*, where he met and befriended T. S. Eliot. After graduation, he worked briefly as a newspaper reporter and then began writing poetry and prose and demonstrated a keen interest in psychoanalysis. In 1912, he married Jessie McDonald. They moved to England and had three children but divorced in the 1920s. Aiken remarried, but, like his father, he also suffered from mental problems. His second wife later wrote that she had prevented Aiken's suicide on one occasion, and that many of his problems could be traced back to the murder-suicide of his parents. All the while, Aiken was writing and publishing poetry collections and novels.

In 1930, Aiken was awarded the Pulitzer Prize for a book of his collected poetry simply titled *Selected Poems*. Aiken divorced again and remarried in 1937. He continued moving and settled in Cape Cod. He was haunted by the deaths of his parents and often wondered about his childhood home. He returned to Savannah once in these years, in 1936, worried about how he would feel being so close to where his young life had been so marred by tragedy. Not only did he survive the visit, but he found that he enjoyed it. He even went and saw the home where his parents had died. Of Savannah, he later said, "It was all quite staggeringly beautiful . . . what was apparently lost turns out to be no such thing."

Although his writing garnered prestigious awards, it never gained him widespread fame or fortune. Some critics said his work was not fashionable, suggesting that it may have been a bit too esoteric or learned for readers of popular literature. Aiken even recognized this and told a friend that it was ironic:

Critics were harsh on each new work of his, saying that the latest did not stand up to the excellent standards of his previous works. Nothing he wrote ever hit the bestseller lists, however. His biographer summed him up as "one of the country's best-known, least read poets and men of letters."

Aiken had friends who were writers, many of whom were as tormented as he was. One of them, Malcolm Lowry, wrote *Under the Volcano* during a time when Aiken visited him in Mexico. *Under the Volcano*, published in 1947, became one of the most acclaimed novels in the English language and included references to Aiken. In 1954, Aiken was given the National Book award for a book titled *Collected Poems*. As Aiken's career progressed, his writing became more introspective and often focused on themes of psychoanalysis. Many considered his 1952 work *Ushant* to be the pinnacle of his career. An "autobiographical novel," it described the life Aiken had led, writing and dealing with his own demons.

As the years went by, Conrad began thinking more fondly of Savannah. He wrote, "Born in that most magical of cities, Savannah, I was allowed to run wild in that earthly paradise until I was nine; ideal for the boy who early decided he wanted to write." In 1962, Conrad moved back to Savannah and bought the house next door to the one where he had lived when his father had killed himself and his mother. His new home was 230 Oglethorpe; his childhood home was 228 Oglethorpe.

In March 1973, Jimmy Carter, then governor of Georgia, named Aiken poet laureate of Georgia. One day, Conrad was visiting a local cemetery and saw a ship pass by on the Wilmington River named the *Cosmos Mariner*. He was so intrigued by the name that he looked for information on it in the local papers but found nothing. He decided that he would incorporate the phrase into his own epitaph: *Cosmos Mariner—Destination Unknown*. He had the words inscribed on a marble bench he placed at his parents' graves. It also said, *Give my love to the world*. Interestingly, very little was ever written about the ship other than its connection to Aiken. The SS *Cosmos Mariner* was a freighter owned by the Cosmos Steamship Corporation and apparently spent much of its time moving freight up and down both coasts of the United States. When Aiken died on August 17, 1973, he was buried in the family plot with his parents, and the bench became his gravestone.

The Conrad Aiken house—the one he lived in as a boy—was built in 1842 and is 3,936 square feet. It has three bedrooms and two and a half baths. It is three stories tall and made of brick. In 1988 it sold for $122,500. Less than twenty years later, in 2005, it sold for $1,050,000. It is privately owned, although a historical marker across the street identifies the house and tells the story of the boy who lived there.

The Aiken family plot is in the Bonaventure Cemetery, Lot 78, Section H, at the corner of Johnny Mercer Lane and Aiken Lane. The bench Aiken placed at his parents' graveside is famous in its own right. It was featured in the book *Midnight in the Garden of Good and Evil* by John Berendt. There, a character named Miss Harty shares martinis in silver goblets with the story's narrator and explains how she had lived next door to Johnny Mercer when she was young. The Mercer name in Savannah is linked to another murder house, but that is another story altogether.

---

* "Kills His Wife and Commits Suicide," *Moberly (MO) Democrat*, February 28, 1901.

* Edward Butscher, *Conrad Aiken: Poet of White Horse Vale* (1988).

Gruesome and Unsolved— Axe Murders on the Plains

THE VILLISCA AXE MURDER HOUSE

1912

508 East 2nd Street
Villisca, Iowa 50864

About seventy miles southeast of Omaha is the sleepy town of Villisca, Iowa. On June 9, 1912, Josiah Moore and his family—his wife and four children—had invited two young sisters to spend the night in their farmhouse. In the middle of the night, a stranger crept onto the property and found the axe Josiah used to chop firewood. With the axe in hand, the intruder checked the back door to the farmhouse and found it unlocked. Quietly, he entered the house and closed the door behind him. He sneaked into the guest bedroom on the first floor, lifted the axe, and slammed it into the head of one of the young women who had been invited to spend the night. He quickly raised the axe again and struck the other sister lying in the bed. Both were killed instantly. The killings happened so quickly that neither victim cried out. The killer then hit each victim in the head a few more times and went looking to see who else was in the house he could kill. Upstairs, he found more people to victimize. In each bedroom he repeated his actions, chopping and hacking the victims as they slept. When he was done, he went back and double-checked his work, striking the victims again to make sure they were dead. He was so zealous in his actions that he even hit the ceilings in some of the rooms with his axe. Then, as if to tidy up the scene, he went from room to room, pulling the bedsheets up to cover the victims' bodies. In all he had killed eight people: the six Moore family members upstairs, and the Stillinger sisters, the overnight houseguests.

Not in a hurry to make his escape, the killer then went around the first floor of the house and drew all the shades. For the windows that had no drapes, he found whatever loose cloth he could find and covered the windows so that no one could look in and see what had happened. Content that his work was done, the killer left the axe behind, locked the door behind him, and disappeared into the darkness. He took nothing of value from the home. It was one of the bloodiest crimes ever to occur in the United States, and it would never be solved. And the house where these killings took place serves to remind us of an era where axe murders seemingly dominated the national headlines.

^ ^ ^

Josiah Moore was a "prominent businessman," according to the news accounts, and lived in Villisca with his wife and four children. He owned and operated the local John Deere dealership and was by all measures an upstanding member of the community. As far as anyone knew, he had no enemies. Seemingly, his life was the prototype for the good American life: He had a wife and children, a farm, and a thriving business in town. Moore's children were eleven, nine, seven, and six. The day before the killings, Lena and Ina Stillinger had come to town to attend a church event, and Moore allowed them to spend the night of June 9 with his family. Friends of the family, the Stillinger sisters were twelve and eight years old.

On the morning of June 10, a neighbor thought it odd when no one appeared to be stirring at the Moore farm. After all, there were six people living there, and two guests, and the family maintained livestock that needed tending. The farmhouse wasn't that large. It was typical of the era with several rooms on the ground floor and a couple of bedrooms upstairs. It must have seemed cramped with eight people spending the night. The neighbor stood on the porch and knocked on the front door. When the neighbor could not get anyone to answer, her husband also tried and failed. The couple went around the house to look for signs of the occupants but could not see inside; all the windows were completely covered from the inside. All the doors were locked as well. Sensing that something was very wrong, the neighbors went into town and sought help. The city marshal came out to the home and forced the front door when no one answered his knock. Inside, he encountered a horrific scene. Josiah and his wife were the first to be found, hacked to death in their first-floor bed. The Stillinger sisters had also been bludgeoned in their bed. The four Moore children, too, were all found dead, similarly killed. The marshal found the axe covered with blood and hair that was obviously the murder weapon. All eight victims were lying in their beds where they had been sleeping; all eight appeared to have been killed by the same axe.

Investigators went through the house and could not fathom what would cause someone to commit such a vicious crime. They noted the damaged ceiling where the murderer had struck it with the axe while he was in the middle of his murder spree. The amount of blood on the scene was staggering. There was no indication that the victims had put up any struggle or even been aware of what happened to them.

The local militia and the townsfolk headed out to scour the countryside, but who were they looking for? No one had seen anyone unusual near the house. It wasn't even clear when during the night the crime had occurred. It seemed like the killer had simply appeared, killed the victims while they slept, and then vanished after locking the door behind him. As far as anyone could tell, nothing had been taken from the house. After investigators had ruled out robbery, the only possible motive seemed to be revenge. But the Moores didn't have any enemies as far as anyone knew. The local paper noted that Mr. Moore was prominent in "business and social circles." And certainly the churchgoing Stillinger sisters could not have been the target of a revenge killing. Was it simply the random act of a madman?

The coroner, a Dr. Linquist, was called to the scene and arrived around 9:00 A.M. At the time, the law allowed him to convene a coroner's inquest jury to call witnesses and examine the facts and circumstances of any death that had not occurred naturally. He quickly determined that a jury would be helpful, and he called in some men and swore them in to help him investigate. The district attorney was also summoned to the house. When everyone arrived, they all went inside and examined the wide-ranging crime scene. It was horrific. All the victims had been struck repeatedly with an axe. They noted how the killer had pulled up the sheets on the beds to cover the bodies. They saw how the killer had spent time after the murders covering the insides of the windows with cloth so that no one could look in and see the gruesome scene. After several hours of studying the crime scene, the coroner removed the bodies and took them to the local fire station, which acted as a makeshift morgue for the eight victims.

The victims were Lena and Ina Stillinger; Josiah and Sarah Moore; and the Moores' children—Herman, Katherine, Boyd, and Paul.

The next day, the coroner convened the jury and began his inquest, calling over a dozen witnesses. The story unfolded witness by witness. The next-door neighbor who had first noticed how quiet the Moore home had been hadn't seen or heard anything out of the ordinary until she began to wonder about the lack of activity at the house. The next witness was Ed Selley, who worked for Josiah Moore. He had come out to the Moore home and tended to the livestock the morning of the murder but left before the bodies were discovered. The coroner asked him if he knew of any enemies that the Moores might have had. He testified that Josiah Moore had once told him, "I got a brother-in-law that don't like me. Said he would get even with me some time." Selley believed Moore was referring to a man named Sam Moyer but had no other details of the trouble. Even so, these murders seemed to be much more than getting "even" with someone. Just because you don't like someone doesn't mean you go and kill them and their family.

A Dr. Cooper testified that the sheriff had come and gotten him, telling him that the Moores had been murdered. He had accompanied the sheriff and the others when they went into the house to conduct a thorough investigation. He gave graphic details that would later be repeated in the local papers and noted that, in his opinion, the murders had occurred five or six hours before he had arrived a little after 8:00 that morning. He also described how all of the bodies were bludgeoned with the axe and then covered with bedsheets. None of the bedsheets were cut or damaged, indicating that the killer had slain the victims and then covered them. There was also no sign of any struggle and all the victims were lying in their beds; presumably, all of the victims were killed in their sleep. He had found it remarkable that the killer had managed to go from room to room in the house, brutally chopping and killing his victims without waking anyone up.

Another doctor, this one named Williams, said that he was also summoned to the Moore home that day and had met Dr. Cooper at the house. It was Williams who performed medical examinations of the victims at the scene. From his description, it sounded like the killer hadn't just set out simply to kill the occupants of the house. He had set out to brutally slaughter his victims in a fit of evil rage. Some of the victims had their faces and heads so badly beaten they were not recognizable. Even the small children had been savagely mutilated, probably after they were already dead.

Local papers carried in-depth coverage of the investigation, but most of what was printed read like gossip. Although they had more than enough detail about the killings, it became clear fairly quickly that the local authorities were clueless when it came to solving the crime. It was determined that the murder weapon belonged to the Moores and had been taken from their own woodshed. Bloodhounds had been brought into town and had followed a trail from the house to a nearby river, but lost the scent. They found a bloody handkerchief along the way, but authorities could make nothing of it. According to the local papers, authorities were investigating the suggestion that two relatives of Mr. Moore held "deep grudges" against him, but little else was known. Investigators also noted the similarities between this case and one in Ellsworth, Kansas. There, about three hundred miles away, someone had committed a murder by the light of a kerosene lamp. There had been a kerosene lamp in the Moore house as well that appeared to have been used by the killer as he went from room to room. There had also been "two strange men" who had "left hurriedly" from Newmarket, a little over twenty miles away, shortly after someone questioned what they were doing in town. These clues—if they were indeed clues—were all disconnected and did not point the authorities in any particular direction.

Local authorities also thought there might be a connection to a murder that had gained headlines the previous year in Colorado. In Colorado Springs, a "similar crime" had taken the lives of six people; it, too, had involved an axe as the murder weapon. Colorado Springs was over six hundred miles away, however, and no one could see how the two groups of victims might be related aside from the weapon of choice. And axe murders were not that uncommon around this time. There appeared to be nothing more to link the two crimes.

When it came to suspects or motives, the local newspapers offered little more than gossip and speculation. The papers instead filled their reporting with specific and gory details of the murders. The Stillinger girls? "The heads were crushed and fearfully mutilated." The Moores? They had their "heads crushed and almost severed from their necks." Newspaper writers described each room of the house and the victims' injuries graphically. But the death scenes were the only details the authorities understood. They couldn't come up with any actual suspects. That would change, though. Eventually, Villisca authorities would have more than enough people to point at. They just wouldn't be able to convict any of them.

In 1912, the sheriff picked up a suspect named Andy Sawyer. A local railroad construction foreman said that Sawyer had shown up at a work site not far from Villisca on the morning after the murders and asked for a job. The foreman needed workers so badly the man was hired on the spot even though something about him seemed odd. He was wearing a suit, his shoes were muddy, and his pants were soaked up to the knees when he first arrived. And he liked to walk around the work site with an axe, even when an axe wasn't needed. His co-workers got even more worried when they saw him sleeping with the axe in his hands. After his arrest, Sawyer provided an airtight alibi: He had been arrested for something else before the night of the murders and had been sitting in a jail cell more than seventy miles away when the Villisca crimes were committed. The sheriff of Osceola, Iowa, confirmed the story and Sawyer was released.

Then, in 1913, a federal agent announced that he knew who the Villisca murderer was. A man named Henry Lee Moore, who was not related to Josiah Moore and his family, lived in Columbia, Missouri, a little less than three hundred miles from Villisca. His mother and grandmother had been brutally murdered by someone wielding an axe in 1911. Henry Lee Moore was brought to trial for the Columbia murders shortly after the Villisca murders occurred in 1912 and was convicted. He was imprisoned and would finally be paroled in 1956. In the murders for which he was convicted, it was said Moore had draped something over the windows of the house so people could not see inside; he had also used an axe and locked all the doors and windows before leaving.

Amazingly, it appears that the Villisca authorities never investigated Moore even though the crimes for which he was convicted bore striking similarities to the Villisca murders. Instead, local authorities pursued other leads. The police may have been incompetent, or other details of the Columbia murders may not have matched up with those of the Villisca killings.

In 1917, investigators got word of a preacher who had been in Villisca the night of the murders but had left early the next morning. Could he have been the murderer? In 1912, George Kelly had settled in a neighboring county, about forty miles from Villisca, where he had traveled in 1911 for a Presbyterian "Children's Day" event. He was arrested and brought to Villisca. Shortly after, law enforcement announced that he had confessed. He was put on trial and people familiar with Kelly's "confession" stated that it was so absurd that it was obviously the result of coercion. In fact, the prosecution chose to not even use it at the trial. The jury came back and told the court they were unable to reach a verdict. Kelly was tried a second time and this time the jury found him not guilty. Soon after, he and his wife fled the area and disappeared.

The Villisca police weren't the only people trying to solve the case. James Wilkerson, a private detective from the Burns agency, came to town and poked around a bit shortly after the case began to grow cold. One of the most prominent people to be brought into the investigation was a businessman-turned-senator named Frank Jones. Josiah Moore had worked for Jones at one point but then had split off to start his own business. Moore's John Deere dealership competed directly with his former boss's business, and some theorized that this was a motive for Jones to have Moore's family killed. The Burns detective stated it was Jones and his son who were behind the slayings. He claimed they had hired a man named William "Blackie" Mansfield, whose parents and family had also been killed by an axe murderer in Blue Island, Illinois, a little more than four hundred miles to the east, in 1914. Wilkerson believed that Mansfield had committed the axe murders in Colorado Springs, Villisca, and then Blue Island.

In 1916, a grand jury convened to hear Wilkerson's case against Mansfield. Unfortunately for Wilkerson, Mansfield produced work records from Illinois proving his whereabouts at the time of the Villisca axe murders, and he was quickly dismissed as a suspect. After he was dismissed by the grand jury, the papers wrote: "The sheriff placed him in an automobile and drove into the country," treating Mansfield the way one would treat a stray dog that had wandered into town. Mansfield was so upset at being branded a serial killer that he sued Wilkerson for slander and won. He was awarded $2,225 in damages.

As more time passed and various suspects were cleared, the case seemed to be growing cold. Then, in 1931, activity on the case was rekindled. A man in Detroit named George Meyers confessed to the killings. It seemed plausible; he was in jail for burglary and a tipster had sent a letter to the Detroit officials saying he was linked to the killings. After a few hours of questioning, he claimed he had been hired to kill a family in Villisca. He said he was paid $2,000 and then fled the area after completing the job. He had no idea who the people were that he had killed or even why they had been targeted. It had just been another job to him. He was supposedly certain of the details: He had killed six people with an axe in Villisca. The problem was that his math was wrong. There had been eight victims in Villisca. Authorities from Detroit and Villisca compared notes and decided that Meyers's story didn't add up. It is unclear if this was the only reason that the authorities dismissed him as a suspect. It seems odd to discount his story simply because of a mathematical error. Did they really expect an axe-wielding killer to be counting his victims as he slaughtered them? Meyers wound up spending fifteen years in a Michigan prison for his burglary conviction, and as far as anyone knows, he was the last person on the radar of Villisca crime enforcement for the murder of the Moore family and their guests. The case remains officially unsolved.

The house is easy to find today. Out front is a sign that reads: "Villisca Ax Murder House—June 10, 1912." It was built in 1868 and Josiah Moore had bought it in 1903.

Darwin and Martha Linn bought the house in 1994 and decided to remodel the house and return it to its condition and configuration on the night of the murders in 1912. This involved removing modern conveniences like running water and electricity and replacing the furniture with items that would be appropriate to the time of 1912 or earlier. Now, the home is open for tours. Overnight stays are also available but appeal mostly to those who are interested in the paranormal. Reports of spiritual activity in and around the house have been made since the home was restored.

From March through November, tours of the house cost $10 per person; admission for children and seniors is $5. For $428, a group of six can stay overnight in the house unattended. The owners of the home will leave you alone in the house—remember, it has no running water or electricity—and ask you to simply lock up when you leave the next morning. Each additional guest will cost $74.90. The story has also been the subject of several books and documentaries.

* Villisca Ax Murder House, villiscaiowa.com
* "Entire Family Wiped Out When Fiend Visits Home," *Muscatine Journal*, June 10, 1912.

Frank Lloyd Wright's Masterpiece—Turned into a Gruesome Crime Scene

TALIESIN

1914

5607 County Road C
Spring Green, Wisconsin 53588

On August 15, 1914, Martha Borthwick and her two children sat down to lunch on an enclosed porch at Taliesin, the summer home Frank Lloyd Wright had built a few years earlier so he and Borthwick, his lover, could escape the gossip caused by their affair. Taliesin also housed offices for Wright's architectural firm, and next to the porch was a dining room where many of Wright's employees gathered to discuss work. According to legend, one of Wright's groundskeepers, a man named Julian Carlton, quietly went around and locked the doors and windows to these rooms. He then poured gasoline under the door to the dining room and set the house on fire.

He had already told his wife, another Wright employee, to leave the building. In his hands, he held an axe.

As the dining room burst into flames, Julian ran into the porch and attacked Borthwick and her children with the axe. He then hacked at the others as they tried escaping from the burning dining room. Along with Borthwick and her two children, Julian killed four others: three employees and the son of an employee. Two men in the dining room managed to make it clear of the axe-wielding madman and the fire and found help nearby. Julian fled the burning building and hid. Neighbors rallied to put the fire out and then helped the police search the estate. They found Julian hiding underneath one of the other buildings on the property. Wright heard the news and raced back to Taliesin from Oak Park, Illinois; he arrived that evening to what he later called a "devastating scene of horror." News reports of the murders and fire did not mention the doors and windows being locked shut, something that the Taliesin Preservation organization today refers to as a "myth." It seems a minor detail added to such a gory crime, probably added just to make it seem even crueler. Either way, the fire and the murders were all too real.

The murders at Taliesin make the home in Spring Green, Wisconsin, the most architecturally significant murder house in America. Designed by Frank Lloyd Wright and built in 1911, Taliesin—pronounced *tally-ESS-in*—was his summer home. It was a refuge for him, as he had recently left his wife and taken up with Borthwick. The two would escape to the Wisconsin countryside to evade the gossip that had escalated to the point of newspaper editorials condemning the couple for their immoral ways. The Taliesin property also housed Wright's office and working quarters and required a staff and ground crew to operate and maintain.

Frank Lloyd Wright is unquestionably America's most famous architect. Wright was born in 1867 and by the 1890s was working as an architect in Chicago. He did not have a degree in architecture and he probably did not even graduate from high school. Wright simply began working for an architect in Chicago and learned by doing. He started out as a draftsman and then apprenticed as an architect. Soon he was designing buildings and homes for the clients of his employer, as well as creating "bootleg" designs as side jobs without his firm's endorsement. In the early 1890s he started his own firm, and by 1900 his fame was growing as more and more homes were built using his designs.

Wright began exploring some innovative ideas. For example, Wright believed that an architect should consider the place where a building was being constructed and seek harmony between the two. Some of his most iconic work involved structures melded into the landscape, epitomized by his "Fallingwater" home, built atop a waterfall in 1937. The house was constructed on top of the waterfall, with the river flowing under the house before plunging over the edge. Fallingwater was praised by *Time* magazine and eventually became recognized as one of the greatest and most admired works by an American architect. Long before he became famous for being

America's architect, however, he was known for the gossip his private life generated.

It was 1909 when his life took a scandalous turn. Although already married for two decades, he became romantically involved with the wife of a client, Martha "Mamah" Borthwick. She filed for divorce from her husband so she could be with Wright. Wright's wife, however, refused to grant him a divorce. The Wrights' situation was a little trickier: They had six children. Her refusal did not stifle his romance. Even though he was still married, Wright openly traveled to Europe with Mamah. For the time, this was considered quite controversial, and upon their return they discovered that the town gossip had reached a fever pitch. Wright decided it would be best if they moved someplace they could have some privacy. He had spent his childhood summers in Spring Green, Wisconsin, at the home of his mother's father, in a valley that had connections to his family going back quite some time. This side of his family traced its roots back to Wales. When Wright decided to build a home in Spring Green, he chose a hill to place the home upon, and decided to locate the house on the "brow" of the hill, not the center of the hilltop. The placement of the home made it much more architecturally interesting, and to some observers the house looked like it was a natural part of the landscape. Wright chose to name it *Taliesin*, after a Welsh poet whose name translated as "Shining Brow," a nod to the home's placement on the brow of the hill.

The building was huge, and he relocated his offices and staff to the new location from Oak Park. Within two years, he was living in Spring Green with Borthwick and conducting his business there. Mamah had quickly obtained her divorce, but Wright was still having problems exiting his marriage. His wife, Catherine, would not consent to a divorce until 1922. Still, Wright and Borthwick settled into the spectacular home and began their new life together. The interior of the home was more than twenty thousand square feet; counting the courtyards and terraces, it encompassed thirty-seven thousand square feet. Wright oversaw construction of more buildings at the site and also purchased surrounding land whenever it became available. Eventually, the property would include a total of five buildings designed by Wright, scattered over six hundred acres.

The Taliesin complex required quite a bit of maintenance and upkeep, so Wright hired a staff of groundskeepers and servants. Among those he hired were Julian and Gertrude Carlton, a couple from Barbados, who came to work at Taliesin in the summer of 1914. Julian was thirty years old and worked as a butler and handyman at the house, and Gertrude cooked. Some visitors to Taliesin said that Julian displayed a bit of a temper. It is hard to say what brought it about, but according to one account, one of Wright's guests had caused Julian to explode by calling him a "black son of a bitch." In August, the Carltons gave Wright their two weeks' notice that they were going to quit. It was probably for the best, and some suggested that Mamah may have told the Carltons it was time for them to leave. Wright went back to Chicago for a quick business trip. It was then that Julian Carlton committed the murders.

Julian Carlton never explained why he had done what he did. His wife also claimed to have no idea why her husband had snapped. Julian tried killing himself by drinking poison shortly after he was arrested but survived. He then went on a hunger strike in jail and, after seven weeks, managed to starve himself to death.

Wright buried Mamah on the property and rebuilt Taliesin, which he renamed *Taliesin II*. The home would burn again, in 1925, when it was struck by lightning. Wright was home on this occasion but was unable to stop the fire from reducing the living quarters to ashes. Although he was able to rebuild Taliesin II, he lost a large collection of Asian artifacts he had acquired during time he had spent in Japan overseeing the construction of the Imperial Hotel in Tokyo. When the home was rebuilt after the fire, he added another digit to the Roman numerals, making it *Taliesin III*.

Wright built a second home in Arizona that he called *Taliesin West*. When its construction was completed in 1937, Taliesin West became Wright's winter home and Taliesin III remained his summer home.

Wright's Wisconsin home became the focus of pilgrimages by many architects and other luminaries who sought to pay homage to Wright, who had become world renowned for his designs. Many of the visitors became lifelong friends. Buckminster Fuller, Philip Johnson, August Perret, G. I. Gurdjieff, Charles Laughton, Carl Sandburg, and Ayn Rand were among those who stayed there. Rand visited after she had written *The*

Fountainhead, her novel about an architect who battles conformity. Many readers thought the book was based on Wright, although she denied it.

Wright died in 1959. In 1940, he had created the Frank Lloyd Wright Foundation, and it became the owner and caretaker of his properties after his death. In 1973, Taliesin was designated a National Historic Landmark, and efforts are being made to maintain and preserve it.

Today, Taliesin is open to the public. Tours of the grounds are available but the property is privately owned, so visitors need to find out in advance the schedule and availability of tours. Many tours sell out during the summer. The grounds now also contain a bookstore and café. Taliesin is located about an hour west of Madison, Wisconsin. Those interested in learning more about the site and visitor information can visit taliesinpreservation.org.

Not far from Taliesin, the state of Wisconsin erected a historical marker that bears this inscription.

> *Frank Lloyd Wright, Wisconsin-born, world-renowned architect, lived and worked in Wyoming Valley, 6 miles southwest of here, at Taliesin, his home and school for apprentices. In the practice of "organic" or natural architecture, he sought to blend structure with site, to create harmonious surroundings for the occupants, to bring the outdoors indoors, and to use materials naturally.*

Among Wright's many innovations were the pre-fabricated house, gravity heat, indirect lighting, concrete block as an effective building material, and revolutionary engineering concepts such as the earthquake-proof structure. Shortly before his death in 1959 at the age of 90, he designed a mile-high office building.

Colorful non-conformist, believer in beauty, and champion of democracy, he scorned all criticism. "Early in life," he said, "I had to choose between honest arrogance and hypocritical humility. I chose the former and have never seen reason to change."

Taliesin is a remarkably beautiful place and the home is fascinating. The caretakers of it now are quick to point out how insignificant the murders were in the grand scheme of things. True, they were horrific and altered Wright's life immeasurably. But they had nothing to do with the home itself and amount to little more than a footnote in its history.

---

* Taliesin Preservation, Inc., taliesinpreservation.org

Where Only Death
Can Remove a Curse

THE "HEX HOUSE"

1928

1709 Rehmeyer's Hollow Road
Stewartstown, Pennsylvania 17363

On the evening of November 27, 1928, three men called at the home of Nelson Rehmeyer. Rehmeyer's farmhouse was fairly isolated, in a hollow near Stewartstown, Pennsylvania. The men, named Blymire, Curry, and Hess, knew Rehmeyer well and the purpose of their visit was straightforward. They had come to undo a hex they believed Rehmeyer had placed on them. It was a simple matter: All they needed was for Rehmeyer to give them a lock of his hair and his spell book. After all, Rehmeyer was a renowned witch.

Rehmeyer lived alone and was a huge man. And he knew very well what these men were up to. He was not going to give up his spell book or a lock of his hair without a fight. The three men barged into the home to take the things forcefully. Rehmeyer put up a fight. None of the men were armed and the four clashed viciously inside the farmhouse. Rehmeyer fought off his attackers with ferocity. The intruders realized they might have gotten themselves into a situation from which they could not easily extract themselves. One of the men smashed a chair over Rehmeyer's head and knocked him out. The intruders then cut off a lock of his hair and began ransacking the house, looking for Rehmeyer's spell book. They could not find it.

They realized that Rehmeyer was dead. Unsure of what to do next, the men poured kerosene on Rehmeyer's body, lit it on fire, and fled. Rehmeyer's body refused to burn; the fire extinguished itself. The three men ran off into the darkness of the hollow, hoping their actions had removed the hex. While much of this story might sound odd today, none of it seemed unusual to the members of the community, most of whom believed in witchcraft.

In the 1920s, conventional wisdom in parts of Pennsylvania held that most everyday problems could be solved with spells and potions. For example, rats and mice could be ordered to leave one's harvest alone by repeating the following phrase as the first three sheaves of the harvest were placed in the barn:

Rats and mice, these three sheaves I give to you,
in order that you may not destroy any of my wheat.

That incantation would assure that the rodents would not eat any of the grain beyond those first three sheaves. This admonition was one of many written by a man named John George Hohman in his bestselling book on hexes, which would play a large role in one of the spookiest murders in American history.

Murder in America is not all that unusual; what was remarkable in the Rehmeyer's Hollow case was that the perpetrators and the victim all believed in a form of rural magic, as described in a popular book at the time called *Pow-Wows; or, Long Lost Friend*. In this context, the word *powwow* does not bear the typical connotation attributed to it by most people, that is, to gather, to talk, to interact. Here, *powwow* means "to heal." It very well could be that the term was borrowed from the Native American concept of a healer. The book was published in 1820 by Hohman, a German printer who had settled near Reading, Pennsylvania, and collected folk remedies, cures, and hexes from the locals. He added in a few spells he had brought with him from Germany and he had a bestseller on his hands. The first edition of the book was printed in German, but soon English translations were being carried in shirt pockets and sitting on nightstands across Pennsylvania Dutch country.

The little book included all manner of spells and incantations, everything from how to ensure your own safe journey to cures for toothaches and epilepsy. Along with the medicinal remedies it included spells that—if cast properly—would purportedly cause a thief to be frozen in his tracks or allow a person to win a lawsuit through the use of a spell. Not all the spells had good intentions. The book described spells that could be cast to cause bad luck to befall one's enemies. In the decades following the publication of *Long Lost Friend*, the book became a respected text among many Pennsylvania Dutch.

The term *Pennsylvania Dutch* often confuses outsiders. The name—as with many words in their dialect—was altered from the original German. The term was originally the Pennsylvania *Deutsch*, a word meaning "German." The group descended from Mennonites who emigrated from Germany to rural Pennsylvania beginning in the late 1600s. The most well-known members of the Pennsylvania Dutch are the Amish, a religious community that has maintained its traditional dress and lifestyle over hundreds of years. Today, many know them from reality television shows that contrast their simple horse-and-buggy lives with the lifestyles of their modern neighbors.

In 1928, Nelson Rehmeyer lived in a simple two-story clapboard-sided house he built on the side of a hill in Rehmeyer's Hollow, a chunk of land in York County, Pennsylvania, that his family had owned and worked for several generations. Nelson constructed his home next to the log cabin his grandparents occupied. Nelson had a wife, Alice Cora Shaffer, and two daughters, but at the time of his murder he lived alone. Neighbors sometimes referred to the man as a hermit, although his estranged wife and children lived just a mile away.

By all accounts Rehmeyer, a reclusive local farmer, was also a powerful "powwow doctor"—a practitioner of the Pennsylvania Dutch form of healing that some called witch-craft. In the community, anyone considered skilled in pow-wow medicine was considered a witch, regardless of their gender. And for Rehmeyer, the most important guide for him in his doctoring would be his copy of *Long Lost Friend*, whose contents he had mastered. And while he may have spent a lot of time working spells and potions to heal the sick, some peo-ple suspected he used his abilities to cast spells on his enemies.

A former worker on Rehmeyer's farm, John H. Blymire, was also a practitioner of powwow and had been known to effect cures for others until, he said, one day his power simply vanished. He believed his spells were being counteracted by another powwow practitioner's spells, a witch more powerful than himself. He had his suspicions but he was not certain who had hexed him. After he lost his healing powers, he also began to feel sickly and so he did what any self-respecting witch would do: He sought advice from another witch. Not certain of who had hexed him, Blymire could not trust a local witch. He went and found one a little ways away from Rehm-eyer's Hollow and described his predicament. The witch told him that his problems were indeed caused by a hex and that she knew how to reveal the identity of the hexmeister. She told Blymire to place a dollar bill in his left hand and stare at it while she worked some magic on it. Blymire later testified that he saw Washington's portrait replaced by an image of

Rehmeyer. When Blymire told the witch what he had seen, she told him there was only one way to remove the hex: He needed to get his hands on Rehmeyer's spell book and burn it. He then had to get a lock of Rehmeyer's hair and bury it. That, and only that, would remove the hex placed on him by Rehmeyer.

Blymire felt he had no choice. He needed to take the necessary steps to rid himself of the spell. He brought along a friend—a fourteen-year-old named John Curry who also believed he had been cursed by Rehmeyer—and went to pay a visit to Rehmeyer. The two pretended to simply be stopping by for a friendly visit. Not knowing that his two callers might intend to harm him, Rehmeyer invited them in and Blymire and Curry even spent the night at Rehmeyer's house when it got too late for them to head home in the darkness. They did not take any action that night, however, because they noticed one problem. Rehmeyer was huge and the men didn't think they could tackle him without help. Still, they remained convinced Rehmeyer was the one who had hexed them.

The next day, Blymire and Curry recruited a third man to help them named Wilbert G. Hess. Amazingly, Hess also blamed Rehmeyer for a recent streak of bad luck and ill health. In this place and time, many people blamed bad luck and ill health on hexes. On the evening of November 27, 1928, the day after Blymire and Curry had spent the night in Rehmeyer's home, the three went to Rehmeyer's house. They were convinced they could counter all of Rehmeyer's hexing by taking his copy of *Long Lost Friend* and getting a lock of his hair. It was this evening that the men attacked Rehmeyer, ransacked his house, and attempted to burn his body.

The men had not originally intended to kill Rehmeyer as far as anyone knew, but the confrontation had spun out of control so quickly that it was probably impossible for it to end in any way without someone dying. The ferocious and deadly struggle made a mess of the house. Furniture was displaced and broken, and blood was splattered everywhere. As Rehmeyer lay dying, the men ransacked his house, looking for Rehmeyer's spell book. They also found a small amount of money in the house, which they took. The attackers then put his lifeless body on a mattress and doused it in kerosene, which they ignited before fleeing the scene. They hoped that the ensuing fire would burn the house down and make it look like Rehmeyer had simply died in a house fire.

Legend has it that the murder was committed at exactly one minute past midnight, but such precision seems unlikely in light of the mayhem that preceded the death. Perhaps the most mysterious aspect of the murder was how Rehmeyer's body did not burn. The fire extinguished itself and the house did not catch fire. Many locals knew that *Long Lost Friend* closed with the admonition: *Whoever carries this book with him, is safe from all his enemies, visible or invisible; and whoever has this book with him cannot die . . . nor burn up in any fire.* Even in death, Rehmeyer's magic was powerful. He didn't have a copy of the book on him, but he was so familiar with it that it protected him anyway. Rehmeyer's body was found the next day by a neighbor who was passing by and wondered why the Rehmeyer place was so quiet. When he approached the back door of the house, the neighbor spotted Rehmeyer's charred body lying on the floor.

Local authorities had no trouble solving the crime. They asked his wife—who lived nearby—if she had any idea who might have harmed her husband. The day of the murder the three men had come by her place and asked her where her husband could be found. She had suggested they go to the house. She recognized Blymire as a previous employee of Nelson's.

The three hadn't tried running away and were quickly arrested. The men also quickly admitted to their roles in the event. Fourteen-year-old Curry gave the police a full written confession in which he described the details of the killing. The earliest press reports did not mention the role witchcraft had played in the crime, but that soon changed.

While the men sat in jail waiting for official charges to be lodged against them, the coroner and an official from the state department of health held a conference on combating the practice of witchcraft. According to the coroner, "several children" had died recently after being treated by "powwow doctors." One source said the number of dead children was five. They hadn't been murdered; they had simply died because their parents took them to someone like Rehmeyer rather than to a medical doctor. York County believed in witchcraft at that time.

The officials appeared to be more than a little confused on how to combat the widespread belief. They passed a resolution asking the local medical society to do what it could to help stamp out the practice. Of course, the powwow "doctors" were not members of the society so it was unclear what the society could do but wring its hands and complain. In the end, it decided that the best way to stop the practice of witchcraft was through education. Local newspapers such as the *Altoona Mirror* reported that the society would sponsor meetings to "educate the people of the county against the witch doctors."

The random deaths of a few children would not be what brought national attention to the widespread practice of witchcraft in this part of Pennsylvania. It would be the trials of these three men. In court, Blymire, Curry, and Hess entered not-guilty pleas to the charge of murder. They never denied killing Rehmeyer; they said they honestly believed they had every right to take action against Rehmeyer in light of the hexes he had placed on them. In essence, it was self-defense. The men were held without bail.

While awaiting trial, Blymire gave an interview to a reporter. Not realizing that his belief in witchcraft made him sound silly to most people outside the area, he told the reporter that killing Rehmeyer had its desired effect. It lifted the hex. "Rehmeyer is dead; I no longer feel bewitched. I now can eat and sleep." The reporter noted that of the three killers, only Curry seemed to show any remorse for what the men had done. Other reporters wondered how the men would be treated by a jury chosen from the area: Many in the jury pool would undoubtedly be believers and practitioners of powwow as well.

Blymire, Curry, and Hess faced their murder charges in three separate trials. The men each testified and admitted they had gone to Rehmeyer's house in an attempt to counter hexes they believed he had placed on them. Blymire's attorney argued to the jury that his client was insane and suggested that his belief in witchcraft was evidence of his insanity. "Blymire was suffering from a particular type of insanity from which there is no relief. He has an honest belief in the powers of witchcraft." It was an interesting argument to make to a jury of Blymire's peers; as the newspapers had predicted, some members of the jury had admitted they believed in powwow magic and found the defense argument insulting. The judge appeared to agree when he made headlines and ruled that believing in witchcraft did not make a person insane. It is unclear whether the jury considered a fact which was published in the papers: Before the murder, Blymire had spent time in the "Harrisburg state hospital for the insane." He had been discharged after they had deemed him "cured." No mention was made in the paper as to whether the stay at the hospital had anything to do with Blymire's belief in witchcraft.

In the trials of Blymire and Curry, the prosecution argued that the witchcraft angle was a canard and that the men had simply gone to Rehmeyer's house to rob him. Admittedly, they

had taken ten or eleven dollars in cash they found while looking for Rehmeyer's copy of *Long Lost Friend*. In the trial of
Wilbert Hess, the prosecution dropped the robbery motive
and simply went with the witchcraft argument. Regardless of
whether someone believed in witchcraft, no one is allowed to
kill someone because of it. In the case against Hess, both of
his parents testified in his defense. His mother swore on the
stand that she had also been cursed by Rehmeyer, and that
the hex was still upon her while she was testifying even
though he was dead. She admitted she had given her son permission to go to Rehmeyer's but only to get the lock of hair
and the spell book. His father told the jury he had also been
hexed. "I felt as though my flesh was being boiled continually.
It was enough to drive a man crazy."

Extensive news coverage of the trial focused on the witchcraft theme, with reporters from around the country taking
notes and firing off dispatches to the farthest corners of the
nation. Even *Time* magazine gave it page space, with an article titled "Crime: Hex & Hoax." The article did not paint the
participants in a particularly flattering light. One witness was
quoted, testifying, "Rehmeyer done it," referring to the hex.
Time ridiculed the backward ways and beliefs of the people
from this little corner of America, simply by publishing quotes
from actual testimony. Blymire's mother, with the mellifluous
name Babulla, told the court, "Yes, John was hexed. But who
done it? You can't tell that. There's so many witches around."
Blymire's father also testified. "Dere was de old time and

now's de new time. In de old time, nobody had no learnin'. Now in de new time, children get A.B.C." Other news outlets covered the trials, detailing the practice of witchcraft in twentieth-century America. The consensus of reporters who covered the story and interviewed locals was that there were hundreds of powwow witch doctors in the area surrounding Rehmeyer's hollow at the time of the trial.

All three men were found guilty. Surprisingly, eighteen-year-old Hess was only found guilty of second-degree murder, but Blymire and Curry, the younger accomplice, were found guilty of first-degree murder. It is possible the jury bought the story that Hess had been motivated by a desire to help his parents, who had claimed to be victims of Rehmeyer's hexes. After the verdict in his case, Hess went to the jury box and shook hands with each member of the jury that had just found him guilty. As he was being led away his mother said, "Be a good boy, Wilbert."

Blymire would spend twenty-four years in prison; the other two would spend only ten each for their roles. While in prison, John Curry began to paint. Soon, his accomplishments with a paintbrush drew enough attention to his cause that people began advocating for his early release from prison so that his talent could be developed. In 1934, just a few years into his sentence, a former Philadelphia district attorney named Charles Fox even championed the cause of Curry. It made the local papers but was not enough to get him out of prison.

After the murder, the Rehmeyer "hex" house remained vacant for some time. One of Rehmeyer's daughters, Gertie Beatrice, married Kenneth Ebaugh and the two of them cleaned the place up a bit to see if they could rent it out. They tore down their grandparents' cabin during the renovation. The house is currently owned by Rickie Ebaugh, great-grandson of Rehmeyer.

Out of context, the house is not all that remarkable and looks like many other simple structures scattered throughout Pennsylvania Dutch country. It is a two-story home that has a noticeable lean to one side; in recent years it was in need of fresh paint. The carpet has been torn up to reveal the spot in the floor where Nelson's killers had tried to burn his body; the floorboards are still scorched. The house is currently not open to the public but it can be seen from the road. It is 828 square feet and has two bedrooms and one bathroom. It sits on a rather large lot, which is 577,000 square feet. A tax assessment in 2011 placed the home's value at $161,000.

In 2013, the current owner—Rehmeyer's great-grandson Rickie Ebaugh—began giving "Hex House" historic hayride tours of the area and of the house in October. The hayrides did not run past Halloween. An event organizer told a reporter that the only complaint he had gotten about the tours was that they weren't scary enough. He explained, "It's a historic hayride tour, it's not a haunted hayride."

A movie called *Apprentice to Murder* was released in 1988 based loosely upon the facts of the Rehmeyer murder. It stars Donald Sutherland and did not do too well at the box office.

Experts suggest that it may have been inspired by the story but is in no way an accurate portrayal of what really happened in Rehmeyer's Hollow. At least two books have been written on the murder, including *The Trials of Hex* by J. Ross McGinnis and *Hex* by Arthur H. Lewis. Meanwhile, there are still people in the area who keep copies of *Pow-Wows; or, Long Lost Friend* handy. Just in case they need to cast a hex or remove one cast by a neighbor.

* "Crime: Hex & Hoax," *Time*, January 21, 1929.

* "York County Will Halt Witchcraft," *Altoona (PA) Mirror*, December 5, 1928.

* John George Hohman, *Pow-Wows; or, Long Lost Friend* (1820).

* Julia Hatmaker, "'Hex Hollow' Murder House Opens to Tours," *Patriot News*, October 26, 2013.

The Murder House Immortalized by *In Cold Blood*

THE CLUTTER FARMHOUSE

1959

Oak Avenue
Holcomb, Kansas 67851

Outside Holcomb, Kansas, Oak Avenue veers sharply to the south after taking travelers west out of town. Those who ignore the turn find themselves on the long tree-lined driveway to the River Valley Farm. In 1959, Herbert Wesley Clutter, forty-eight, lived there with his wife, Bonnie Mae, forty-five, and two teenaged children on a wheat farm on the outskirts of town. Two other adult children had moved out of the home. The setting was idyllic until two uninvited visitors shattered the peace in the early morning hours of November 15 of that year. Richard Hickock and Perry Smith, two recent prison inmates, broke into the home and told Clutter they were there to rob him. The men were wearing rubber gloves and carrying rope and tape they had bought earlier that day. Clutter informed them he did not keep cash in the house. The burglars did not believe him. They put the family members in separate rooms and tied them up. They then ransacked the house. The hardened criminals found less than $50 and realized Clutter had told them the truth: There was no safe in the house. Hickock and Smith also knew they would go back to prison for a long time if they were caught after this burglary and armed robbery. They decided to kill Herb Clutter and everyone else in the home. They slit the father's throat and then shot him in the head with a shotgun. They then went from room to room and killed the other members of the Clutter family, each with a shotgun blast to the head. They left the house having been there only an hour.

Although many people may not recognize the house at the end of the drive today, it was the epicenter of one of the most famous crime stories in twentieth-century America. It all started on November 16, 1959, when the *New York Times* ran a short piece on the horrific crime that had shaken the little community of Holcomb, Kansas, the day before. Apparently, a newswire service had picked up the story and distributed it to papers far and wide.

Wealthy Farmer, 3 of Family Slain

A wealthy wheat farmer, his wife, and their two young children were found shot to death today in their home. They had been killed by shotgun blasts at close range after being bound and gagged. The father, 48-year-old Herbert W. Clutter, was found in the basement with his son, Kenyon, 15. His wife, Bonnie, 45, and a daughter, Nancy, 16, were in their beds. There were no signs of a struggle and nothing had been stolen. The telephone lines had been cut. "This is apparently the case of a psychopathic killer," Sheriff Earl Robinson said.

The three-hundred-word piece was buried in the back of the *New York Times*, but it caught the eye of New York writer Truman Capote. Capote was thirty-five and had recently found success with short stories and novels, most notably by this time *Breakfast at Tiffany's*. He found the *New York Times* article jarring. How could such a thing happen in small-town America? To answer that question, Capote would study the murders and eventually write a groundbreaking book. He persuaded his publisher to support him while he pursued what would end up being a six-year project, immersing himself in the community of Holcomb and getting to know everyone and everything there was to know about the murders. He would even befriend the killers and mourn their executions.

Capote hoped the case would prove compelling enough for him to write a "nonfiction novel" based on the story of the murders. That is, a book that was a true story, but written in the story-telling style of a novel. He enlisted the help of a childhood friend, Harper Lee, who later found fame after writing *To Kill a Mockingbird*. The two traveled to Holcomb to study the case, and Capote's book, *In Cold Blood*, would become a bestseller. Capote soon learned all the details of the Clutter family and how they came to such a gruesome end in small-town America.

In 1959, Herb Clutter lived with his wife, Bonnie, and two teenaged children on the wheat farm on the outskirts of Holcomb. At the time, the town of Holcomb was home to fewer than three hundred people. Clutter had built the house in 1948 and ran a successful farming operation that encompassed a thousand acres around the home. His operation was so large, he often employed more than a dozen workers. One of his workers, Floyd Wells, would later spend time in prison. While there, he told a fellow inmate that Clutter kept a safe full of cash at his farm. It is unclear why Wells told him this: Clutter had never kept a safe at the farm and was actually known to conduct most of his business using checks because it was easier for his bookkeeping. It very well could be that Wells was just telling wild stories to pass the time behind bars. The inmate who heard the story, Richard Hickock, believed the story and decided it would be "the perfect score."

When Hickock got out of prison, he recruited a former cellmate named Perry Edward Smith to help him with the caper, and the two headed to Holcomb. The farm was easy to find and distinctive enough for them to know they had the right place. The men cut the telephone line going into the house. They then sneaked in while the family slept and bound and gagged the four occupants of the house. They had a shotgun and a knife and ordered Clutter to show them the safe. Clutter told them there was no safe and that all he had was a small amount of cash, which he offered to give to the men. Hickock and Smith now found themselves in a bad situation. Hickock was hoping to steal enough money to start a new life in Mexico. Instead, he was going to have to flee an armed robbery empty-handed. They also knew they would end up back in prison soon if they left any witnesses to their failed robbery. Smith panicked and slashed Herb Clutter's throat. He then shot him in the head. The men went room to room and killed the three remaining members of the family by shooting them in the head once each with a shotgun. The men then fled. Their total haul from the robbery was $40 in cash, some binoculars and a radio.

News of the horrific murders soon spread across the country. Still sitting in his prison cell, Wells heard the news and immediately remembered telling Hickock about the Clutter farm and the safe; he knew Hickock had to be one of the killers. He contacted the warden and told him to let the authorities know to be on the lookout for Hickock. Hickock and Smith were picked up in Las Vegas on December 30, 1959.

The two were brought back to Kansas and were tried for the murders. The two claimed indigence and were given court-appointed attorneys. Counsel immediately sought determinations of whether the two might be able to plead insanity.

Pursuant to Kansas law, the court had the two examined by independent medical experts, and each was deemed fit to stand trial.

The trial did not go well for the men. Authorities told the court how the two men had been their own worst enemies when it came to keeping their actions secret. Once they had been arrested, the two told the police everything. They had disposed of their getaway car in Mexico City, along with the binoculars and the radio they had stolen from the Clutter house. Authorities managed to go to Mexico City and recover these items. The men had buried some of the evidence by the roadside miles from the crime scene. Again, the men told the police where to dig to find the incriminating evidence. By the time the prosecution got halfway through with its case, it was apparent that the trial was little more than a formality. The evidence against Hickock and Smith was overwhelming. A psychiatrist called as an expert for the defendants even admitted that Hickock knew right from wrong at the time of the killings. The high point of the trial for the defense may have been when the same psychiatrist said he simply had no opinion as to Smith's understanding of right and wrong.

Capote had come to town to begin his investigation and sat through the trial, taking thousands of pages of notes. He also schmoozed many of the townspeople and became a fixture in the local community. The jury found the men guilty of the murders and sentenced them to death. The two filed appeals and spent five years on death row while their appeals wound through the system. While doing his research, Capote befriended the killers and much of his book would include portions of his jailhouse interviews, in which the convicted killers said the most remarkable things. Smith told Capote in one particularly striking passage, "I didn't want to harm the man. I thought he was a very nice gentleman. Soft spoken. I thought so right up to the moment I cut his throat."

Capote found the men fascinating, particularly Perry Smith. Smith's tragic life seemed a foregone conclusion, as if he had been destined from childhood to be a criminal and to hang for his misdeeds. He had spent time in orphanages and street gangs. The life of crime seemed to Capote to be inevitable for Smith. Yet on death row, Smith wrote poetry and painted. Using watercolors and bedsheets, he painted seascapes and religious images and gave them to the prison chaplain. In Capote's hands, the stories of the two men seemed Shakespearean and the killers became human, not just monsters from newspaper headlines.

The men were hanged in the early morning hours of April 14, 1965, in Lansing, Kansas. Capote had originally planned to watch the executions as sort of the last chapter of his personal journey, but he couldn't bring himself to attend the event. He had grown too fond of the men to watch them die. However, the deaths allowed Capote to finally end his book. Up until the Supreme Court denied the killers' final appeal, Capote wasn't sure himself how his nonfiction novel was going to end.

Capote finished his book and submitted it to his publisher.

The work was considered a masterpiece and was almost universally applauded. The story was serialized in the *New Yorker* over four issues in 1965 and was a huge hit. Random House published the complete book in January 1966 and it became an instant bestseller. The book was eventually turned into two films, one of which was partially filmed on location in the Clutter house. That version, the first of the two, was nominated for four Academy Awards. Films have also been made about Capote's life, which included depictions of his travels to Holcomb and the writing of *In Cold Blood*. Still, not everyone was happy with Capote's telling of the story. The two surviving Clutter daughters complained that Capote had not spoken with the family and friends of the Clutters, who could have given him a clearer picture and allowed him to portray the victims in a more favorable light. They issued a statement that was widely publicized. "The result was his sensational novel, which profited him and grossly misrepresented our family." Many people were also unhappy with Capote's sympathetic portraits of the killers. By focusing so much on them and their lives, some readers thought Capote was trying to downplay the crimes they had committed.

Meanwhile, Hickock and Smith would not rest in peace. In 2012, law enforcement officials obtained permission to exhume their bodies as part of a murder investigation in Florida. In December 1959, the Walker family of Osprey, Florida, had been murdered. The seemingly random murders had baffled investigators. The four members of the family were all shot, and one of them was raped. Hickock and Smith were on the run after the Clutter murders, and some people believed they may have traveled to Florida during that time. The police gathered evidence but the testing techniques in 1959 did not reveal anything useful. But more recent advances in DNA analysis may allow for it. So the exhumation was ordered, to see if the case could be finally closed. Authorities opened the graves and recovered bone fragments and then reinterred the two in the cemetery near Lansing, Kansas. To date, the results of the DNA testing have not been released.

The Clutter house is approximately 3,600 square feet, not counting its large basement. It is two stories and has five bedrooms and three baths; it currently sits on only seven acres of the original 1,000-acre farm. When Herb Clutter built it in 1948, he said it had cost him $40,000 to construct. It has hardwood floors on both stories and fireplaces in the living room and basement. The basement added another 1,700 square feet.

Bob Byrd bought the house after the Clutter murders and sold the house to the Mader family in 1990. So many people were still making the trek to look at the house that the Maders began giving tours of the house and charging visitors $5. In 2006 they put the house up for auction, but the bids never reached their minimum and they took the house off the market. They were hoping for $200,000—it appraised in the range of $200,000 to $300,000—but the highest bid received was reportedly in the range of $100,000. In 2006, the county appraised the house for tax purposes at $160,390. As with many murder houses, there are stories that the house is haunted. Particularly enduring is the story that Nancy, the daughter who was sixteen years old at the time of the murders, still haunts the house. Currently, the house is privately owned and not open to the public.

* Truman Capote, *In Cold Blood* (1966).

* Ralph F. Voss, *Truman Capote and the Legacy of* In Cold Blood (2011).

* "Wealthy Farmer, 3 of Family Slain," *New York Times*, November 16, 1959.

Born to Raise Hell

RICHARD SPECK

1966

2319 East 100th Street
Chicago, Illinois 60617

One of America's most infamous murderers from the latter half of the twentieth century was Richard Franklin Speck. Speck was an unemployed twenty-four-year-old drifter who spent some time working on ships in the Great Lakes. Around 11:00 P.M. on July 13, 1966, Speck walked up to the back door of a town house at 2319 E. 100th Street on the south side of Chicago. The town house was on the end of an apartment complex with six units, side by side. It was only a few hundred feet from the merchant marine union hall, and he probably noticed it from his time spent on the streets there recently. This particular town house was home to eight young women—nursing students from South Chicago Community Hospital—and they had another female friend staying with them that evening. Speck had a knife and a gun he had stolen from a woman he had raped earlier that evening. Unquestionably, Speck was a very bad man. He had *Born to Raise Hell* tattooed on his arm, with *LOVE* across one set of knuckles and *HATE* across the other.

Speck forced his way into the town house and herded the women into a bedroom at gunpoint. He then tied them up. Somewhere along the way, he missed one young woman. A nurse named Corazon Amurao crawled under the bottom mattress of a bunk bed and hid when she first heard the commotion at the back of the apartment. From her vantage point under the bed, she watched as Speck took the women out of the room one at a time. A while later, he would return and get another. She would later learn that Speck was raping the women and strangling and stabbing them to death. The victims who were strangled had distinctive knots tied in the material they were strangled with—which would make a lot of sense to investigators later when they discovered that their suspect was a sailor. He raped one of them in the same room where Amurao was hiding beneath the bunk bed. After he had killed the eight women—over a period of four and a half hours—Speck left the apartment. The entire time, Amurao hid beneath the bed, waiting for the ordeal to end. Around sunrise, Amurao emerged from under the bed and saw her dead roommates. She climbed out a window and started yelling for help. "They're all dead! All my friends are dead!" Neighbors called the police.

A local radio reporter named Joe Cummings was out driving nearby when he heard the call over the police radio, and he raced to the location. Encountering just one police officer at the apartment, Cummings entered the town house and wandered around the crime scene, seeing the bodies of the victims and noting the large amount of blood on the floor—which he walked through. He then called in to WCFL with his mobile radio equipment and did some live broadcasts from the scene, announcing to Chicago that eight nursing students had been murdered at his location. More police soon arrived. Cummings continued his reporting, helping keep Chicago on high alert as the people of the city realized a crazed murderer was on the loose.

Police soon found the fingerprints of the killer at the scene. Detectives had also gotten a good description from Amurao: the killer was tall, had blond hair, and spoke with a heavy southern accent. Police fanned out and began questioning everyone they could find nearby. People in the neighborhood remembered seeing the man described by Amurao in the area recently. The nearby union hall appeared to be part of the puzzle. Might a sailor have spotted the boardinghouse filled with nurses when he came and went from the hall? Sure enough, someone at the hall remembered a sailor matching the description given by Amurao. The man had been upset about not getting a job and had made a scene. The event had stuck in the clerk's mind, and he could remember the angry man's name. His name was Richard Speck. And Speck had previously given his fingerprints to try to get a job; it was just a matter of time before the police would catch him.

Richard Franklin Speck was born in 1941 and had an ugly upbringing in a large family with an alcoholic and violent stepfather. He also had a short-lived marriage that ended when his wife divorced him, saying he had regularly raped her. He spent time in prison in Texas and on another occasion paid a $10 fine after stabbing someone. In 1966, Speck headed north to see if a change of scenery might help. His sister Martha lived in Chicago and he would stay with her and her husband, Gene Thornton, until he wore out his welcome. Speck was the kind of guy who was always in, near, or causing trouble. It didn't take long for his brother-in-law to figure that out.

Speck's brother-in-law had been in the navy and thought Speck should get a job as an apprentice seaman onboard a ship. If nothing else, it would get Speck out of their lives for long periods of time. Who knows? Maybe Speck would find someplace far away that he liked better than Chicago. The two went into the Coast Guard office and Speck applied for a letter of authority, which would allow him to get an entry-level job on board a Great Lakes ship. The process required Speck to provide fingerprints and to have his picture taken. He then landed a job on an iron ore freighter working the Great Lakes. His first trip didn't go smoothly; he developed appendicitis and had to be airlifted from the boat to Hancock, in Michigan's Upper Peninsula. He rejoined the ship but got in a drunken argument on board and was kicked off. He wound up back at his sister's place.

His brother-in-law wasn't going to give up on his dream of getting Speck out of the house. He took Speck to the National Maritime Union hiring hall so he could file the necessary paperwork to obtain his seaman's card. Speck then tried getting aboard another ship but ran into a stretch of bad luck. Several positions were filled shortly before he heard of them, and at least once he was sent on a wild-goose chase after a job that had already been filled. After one of these fruitless attempts at getting a job he caused a ruckus, yelling at one of the agents for the union. The agent would remember the incident.

Meanwhile, Speck was staying with his sister and brother-in-law, but it was clear that they were getting tired of having him around. They finally told him he had to leave. Speck spent a night or two on the streets, sleeping in houses that were still under construction and drinking at local dive bars. The last time his sister saw him before the trouble was in the parking lot of the union hall, at 2335 E. 100th Street in Chicago.

On July 13, Speck spent the day drinking in a local bar and spotted a woman there named Ella Hooper who was also drinking. He lured her back to a cheap hotel room, where he raped and robbed her. One of the things he stole from her was a small pistol that she had been carrying in her purse. He then went back out, had dinner, and returned to the bar where he had encountered Hooper. He drank some more. It was at that point he went to the apartment filled with nursing students, armed with the gun he had stolen from Hooper.

Amazingly, after his killing spree, Speck didn't run far. Even though he knew he was a wanted man, Speck didn't leave Chicago and spent the next few days hanging around cheap hotels and drinking in local bars. The police found the address of Speck's sister and brother-in-law on paperwork he had left with the union, and they asked the union to call to say that they had found a job for Speck. The brother-in-law managed to find Speck quickly and told him to call the union hall. When he called, they told him that a job was available on a ship that Speck knew had sailed a few days earlier. It was one of the ships he had been angry about when he wasn't hired. Suspecting a trap, Speck told them he was out of town but he would see what he could do about getting to Chicago.

Still, he did not act like a fugitive. He brought a prostitute back to his room and even told her his name was Richard. When she left the room, she alerted the front desk to the fact that Speck had a gun. The police showed up and questioned him. They asked for identification, but the name did not mean anything to them yet. Amazingly, investigators at the scene of the murders had learned Speck's identity, but they had not gotten word to all of their patrolmen yet. The police took his gun and left. Recognizing how lucky he had just been, Speck quickly changed hotels, moving to another—one that charged only eighty-five cents a night. Police finally got word out about their suspect to their patrol officers and the media. News reports soon included Speck's name and a good description of his distinctive *Born to Raise Hell* tattoo. Chicago became a city on edge.

Speck realized now his time was limited; he had bought newspapers that prominently displayed his picture and name on the front page, saying he was wanted for murder. Speck went back to his eighty-five-cents-a-night hotel and attempted to commit suicide by slashing his wrists with a broken wine bottle. The desk clerk at the hotel was alerted by a fellow tenant who saw Speck bleeding and called an ambulance. At Cook County Hospital, one of the doctors attending to Speck noticed the *Born to Raise Hell* tattoo and remembered reading about it in the papers. The police were on the scene shortly. They talked Amurao into putting on her nurse's uniform and going on rounds with another nurse from the hospital, to see if Speck was the right man. After seeing him again face-to-face, she confirmed it. Chicago police were overly cautious, not wanting to possibly make any mistakes with the arrest of such an infamous killer.

Speck claimed to not remember anything about the night of the murders. He said he had been drinking and on drugs and the entire night was blank in his memory. No one bought it. The state had Speck examined by a team of psychiatrists and doctors to make sure he was competent to stand trial, and they confirmed that he was mentally sound.

Speck had little chance of acquittal. Along with his fingerprints at the scene and his checkered past, there had been the one witness: Cora Amurao. It took the jury only forty-nine minutes to find him guilty. The court sentenced him to death. After a series of appeals, Speck's death sentence was overturned by the U.S. Supreme Court, which found that the court had improperly let the prosecution exclude people from the jury pool who had been opposed to the death penalty. Shortly after that, the U.S. Supreme Court declared the death penalty unconstitutional anyway. Speck was then resentenced: His term would be from four hundred to twelve hundred years in prison. He wouldn't live that long. He died of a heart attack shortly before his fiftieth birthday, in 1991.

Before he died, however, Speck made some more headlines from behind bars. In 1978 he granted an interview to Chicago newspaper columnist Bob Greene. He no longer claimed to have had amnesia at the time of the killings. He openly admitted that he had killed the eight women and he remembered it quite well. He told Greene he passed his time in prison getting high on drugs and believed he would be out of prison before the year 2000. Readers were angered and wondered how prisoners were getting drugs while behind bars. That wouldn't be the last time Speck made headlines.

Someone shot a video in 1988 of Speck in prison and passed the video along to a Chicago television reporter named Bill Kurtis in 1996. On camera, Speck spoke casually of how he had killed the women—"It just wasn't their night"—but his behavior on camera was what shocked its viewers. Speck walked around in silk panties and had apparently grown breasts. People speculated that he had somehow gotten his hands on hormones while behind bars. He also ingested cocaine and performed oral sex on another inmate while on camera. The entire time, it was clear that Speck knew he was being videotaped and didn't care. He appeared to believe he could do anything he wanted and get away with it. On camera he said, "If they only knew how much fun I was having, they'd turn me loose." The video caused an even bigger uproar than the Greene column. Who was giving Speck cocaine while behind bars? How was he getting hormone treatments? Was anyone supervising the prisoners? Who gave them a video camera?

The apartment where Speck killed the nurses was eventually turned into a condominium along with the rest of the units in the complex. The town house unit where Speck killed his victims is on the far left of a six-unit block of two-story town houses, as viewed from the street. The individual unit in question sold in 2005 for $89,000 and again in 2005 for $96,000. It is 1,464 square feet with one and a half baths. It was built in 1958. It is now privately owned and is nondescript compared to other murder houses around the country, blending in perfectly with the other units to which it is attached. If it were not pointed out to a passerby, there would be no way of knowing what atrocities had been committed there in 1966.

---

* Bob Sector, "The Richard Speck Case," *Chicago Tribune*, July 13, 1966.

Helter Skelter Houses

THE HINMAN HOUSE
THE TATE HOUSE
THE LABIANCA HOUSE

1969

964 Old Topanga Canyon Road
Topanga, California 90290

10066 Cielo Drive (formerly 10050 Cielo Drive)
Beverly Hills, California 90210
Demolished—new house built on location

3311 Waverly Drive (formerly 3301 Waverly Drive)
Los Angeles, California 90027

In the summer of 1969, a series of bizarre and bloody murders occurred in the Los Angeles area that confounded local authorities. At first, police didn't even spot the links between the murders, which took place at three different locations. A music teacher named Gary Hinman was tortured and stabbed to death at a remote house in Topanga Canyon.

His killer wrote *Political Piggy* on the wall in Hinman's blood. Less than two weeks later, five people were shot and stabbed to death in a bizarre scene, with the word *PIG* written in one victim's blood on the door of the house where the victims were murdered. Several of the victims were well known in show business, including actress Sharon Tate and Jay Sebring, Hollywood's best-known hairstylist. Despite valuables and cash being present, the killer or killers did not bother stealing anything. Another double murder took place the very next day in Los Angeles. Again, nothing connected these victims to the others, but someone had written a bloody message on the wall of this crime scene as well. The police would eventually realize that the victims had all run afoul of a bizarre character named Charles Manson and his followers, the Manson Family.

The thirty-four-year-old music teacher, Gary Hinman, lived about thirty miles west of Los Angeles, in Topanga Canyon. Hinman was known to befriend strangers easily, especially other musicians. Somewhere along the line he met a group of hippies led by a man whose own musical aspirations had not come to fruition. The failed musician and leader of the group was Charles Manson.

Charles Milles Manson was a small-time criminal who had come to California in the mid-1960s. Born in 1934, he had a rap sheet that involved auto theft, check forgery, and pimping by the time he got to California. Once there, he surrounded himself with people who believed that he was messianic and didn't mind breaking the law for him. In the hippie culture of the time, it wasn't hard for him to find followers. There were plenty of people who had drifted to San Francisco looking for answers, and drugs. Manson had plenty of both. He believed that the end of the world was nearing, and he explained to his followers that they would survive the coming apocalypse by following him. His Family members would do anything he asked of them and as time went by, the requests became more and more extreme. Manson's philosophy has been dissected in many books and films and would be impossible to condense here. Suffice it to say that he became convinced that a race war was impending between blacks and whites in America. He was inspired by the song "Helter Skelter," from the Beatles' *White Album,* which he believed contained coded clues supporting his beliefs. The race war was imminent but needed a spark. One thing that might start the ball rolling, according to his way of thinking, would be a well-publicized murder of white people by some blacks. Manson thought he might be able to carry out a murder or two and make it look like the culprits were militant blacks.

The Manson Family did not actually have any regular income, and Manson and his followers managed to survive by seeking handouts when they could find them and stealing when they couldn't. Sometimes they dealt drugs. Manson believed that a musician he knew, Gary Hinman, had come into a large inheritance. Manson asked a few of his disciples, Bobby Beausoleil, Mary Brunner, and Susan Atkins, to go to Hinman's house and get the money from him. It didn't matter how: They would ask for it first but if he didn't give it to them willingly, they were to simply take it. Another story has also been given to explain why Hinman ran afoul of the Family. They claimed he had sold them some bad drugs, which they had in turn resold to a motorcycle gang in Los Angeles. When the gang members demanded their money back, the Family naturally felt they should get a refund from Hinman. Regardless of which reason Manson sent the Family members to Hinman's, the thrust of their visit was clear: They wanted Hinman to give them money.

The three showed up at Hinman's house on Old Topanga Canyon Road and he told them he had no money, inheritance or otherwise. He was probably surprised by how they treated him. Previously, he had let Manson and some of his Family members stay at the house. Unsure of whether Hinman was telling them the truth, they held him captive in his house for a couple of days. When it was clear that Hinman was not going to give them any money, one of his tormentors called Manson and asked for advice. Manson came to the house—carrying a sword—and spoke with Hinman, who continued insisting he did not have any money he could give them. Manson didn't believe him and got angry; he slashed Hinman with the sword to emphasize his point. Hinman still could not furnish them any money. Manson left, after telling Beausoleil and the others to make the killing look like the work of Black Panthers. Beausoleil stabbed Hinman to death and one of the members of the group scrawled *Political Piggy* on the wall with Hinman's blood. This strange murder on July 27, 1969, would baffle local law enforcement, but soon there would be other murders in the news.

Manson hoped that a race war would break out when word of the killing became public, but one failed to commence. It is unclear why Manson believed this murder would launch anything other than a murder investigation. Worse, neither Manson nor any members of his Family were very clever when it came to committing crimes. They were so sloppy, the only reason police didn't catch them sooner was simple incompetence on the part of the police. Bobby Beausoleil was arrested a short while later driving Hinman's car with the murder weapon in the tire well. It was a theme that would often repeat. Members of the Manson clan acted as if they didn't believe or didn't care whether they would ever be caught.

The first Helter Skelter trigger had fizzled and now one of Manson's clan was in jail. Despite the setback, Manson would move ahead with his plans to start the race war. On the evening of August 8, 1969, the Manson Family—without Charles Manson present—committed one of the most gruesome crimes in U.S. history. Manson sent several members of the Family to a home at 10050 Cielo Drive in Beverly Hills. The property sat at the end of a cul-de-sac on the edge of a canyon above Los Angeles. At one time it had been rented by a music producer named Terry Melcher. Melcher had met Manson and had even made several trips to Manson's various haunts to hear songs Manson played on the guitar. Manson was convinced he would someday outsell the Beatles and he believed his music would be prophetic, bringing the message of his weird philosophies to the masses. Apparently Melcher's initial interest had waned and now Manson was upset. Manson had tried to talk to Melcher in March but when he went to the house on Cielo Drive, new tenants there told him that Melcher had just moved out. Not sure if he should believe them, Manson walked around the property and ran into Rudy Altobelli. Altobelli owned the property but lived in the guesthouse out back so he could rent the larger main living quarters to others. Altobelli confirmed that Melcher and his housemate, Candice Bergen, had moved out. Manson recognized Altobelli; the two had met previously and Altobelli was also in the entertainment business. Altobelli told Manson he could not talk any longer as he was packing for a long trip to Europe.

Manson may have felt slighted by Altobelli and the tenants on the property. He may have been upset that Melcher had moved without telling him. Either way, he decided to target the occupants of the home. On August 8, less than two weeks after the Hinman murder but several months after he had first gone looking for Melcher, Manson sent four Family members—"Tex" Watson, Susan Atkins, Linda Kasabian, and Patricia Krenwinkel—to the former Melcher residence and told them to "totally destroy everyone" there. It is unclear if Manson even knew who the current tenants would be when his crew got there. They were film director Roman Polanski and his pregnant wife, actress Sharon Tate. On the night the Manson Family attacked, Polanski was away on business—Altobelli was also away—but Tate had houseguests. One was Jay Sebring, a friend and well-known hairstylist in Los Angeles. Polanski's friend Voytek Frykowski was there, along with his girlfriend, Abigail Folger. Folger was not famous in the Hollywood sense but she was part of the family that had made its fortune selling coffee.

Also unknown to the Manson team was that the house out back—the one Altobelli lived in while renting the main house to others—was occupied by a young man who was watching Altobelli's dogs while their owner was in Europe. William Garretson had been out earlier that evening but returned home. A young man he was friends with dropped by unexpectedly before midnight and the two drank some beer and smoked some marijuana. The visitor was Steve Parent, an eighteen-year-old from El Monte, a suburb east of Los Angeles. It was the unlikeliest of circumstances that led to his presence that evening. Previously, he had picked up Garretson hitchhiking and given him a ride to Cielo Drive. Garretson had told Parent he could drop by if he was ever in the neighborhood. Parent dropped by that night. He was a hi-fi enthusiast—as was Garretson—and had brought over a clock radio he hoped to sell Garretson. Garretson didn't buy it, however.

The Manson Family members approached the Cielo Drive home quietly. The property was surrounded by a tall fence and had an automatic gate that had no security code—simply pressing the button on the box at the gate caused it to open. Tex Watson climbed the telephone pole near the gate and cut the phone lines to the house. The intruders climbed the fence to enter the yard and headed toward the house. It was shortly after midnight.

Walking toward the house, they saw Steve Parent driving toward the gate. Watson waved for him to stop and approached the driver's-side window of the car. Watson shot Parent four times with a .22-caliber handgun. The group then headed to the house. There, Watson cut a screen so he could climb in a window while Kasabian stood watch on the front lawn. Watson then let Atkins and Krenwinkel in through the front door. Frykowski had been sleeping on the couch but was awakened by Watson and asked who he was. "I'm the devil and I'm here to do the devil's business." He kicked Frykowski in the head. The three intruders then rounded up the others in the house and brought them to the living room. They had brought rope with them, which they had apparently planned to use to hang some of the victims. They did manage to tie up a couple of the victims, but Folger and Frykowski each managed to get out of the house. They were chased down and killed on the lawn, beaten and stabbed repeatedly. Sharon Tate and Jay Sebring were gruesomely stabbed to death inside the house.

Tate was stabbed sixteen times, with five stab wounds that would have been fatal by themselves. Sebring was stabbed seven times and shot once. Abigail Folger had been stabbed twenty-eight times. Voytek Frykowski was stabbed fifty-one times, shot two times, and beaten on the head with a blunt object—probably a handgun—thirteen times. One of the killers wrote the word *Pig* on the front door of the house in Tate's blood. The killers then fled, running down the driveway and activating the gate. They sped off into the darkness.

The next day, the housekeeper arrived at the home and noticed the phone lines limply hanging over the fence but thought little of it. She let herself in through the front gate and did not notice that there was a dead body sprawled across the front seat of the strange car in the driveway. She let herself in the back door as was her routine and then walked into the house, where she saw bodies and blood. She had not noticed the bodies of Frykowski and Folger on the lawn. Hysterical, she ran to a neighbor's and asked for the police to be called. Soon, the police and the news media were swarming the area, trying to make sense of it all.

When the four Manson Family members recounted the story later to Manson, he was disappointed in how they had handled the killings. He told them that he would go out with them and show them how such a murder needed to be committed. And the very next day, he did.

Leno LaBianca, forty-four, and Rosemary LaBianca, thirty-eight, owned a beautiful home in Los Angeles on Waverly Drive, a reward for the success of running a lucrative grocery chain. There is some debate as to why Manson chose this house for his next murder. Manson had attended a party at the home next door to the LaBiancas earlier and may have burglarized the house previously. On Sunday, August 10, Manson merely walked up to the back door of the house and let himself in; the door was unlocked. It was approaching 2:00 A.M. Leno and Rosemary were still awake as they had recently returned from a long trip and had gotten home late. Manson tied the two up.

Manson assured the two that he was only there to rob them. More of Manson's Family entered the house to help him. After tying up the LaBiancas and putting pillowcases over their heads, the group of intruders brutally stabbed the two to death. There is no question that Manson entered the house, but most experts agree that he was not physically present within the house when the murders took place. Manson may have mistakenly thought this would relieve him of legal culpability for the murders. Leno LaBianca received twenty-six stab or puncture wounds—some were inflicted by a two-tined serving fork—and Rosemary was stabbed forty-one times. Afterward, someone wrote the words *Healter Skelter* [*sic*], *Rise*, and *Death to pigs* around the house in blood. Someone also carved the word *War* into Leno LaBianca's abdomen.

Amazingly, investigators working on the three murder cases—Hinman, Tate, and LaBianca—did not spot the obvious similarities between the crimes. The LAPD, apparently wanting to keep the public from worrying that there might be crazed lunatics on a killing spree in the area, went so far as to tell the press on August 12 that the Tate and LaBianca murders were unrelated. Some people, hearing that the police had declared the killings unrelated, assumed that the second murders were "copycat" killings. Oddly, almost no one linked the three crimes: Hinman, Tate, and LaBianca.

Public interest in the Tate case was overwhelming, because of the horrific nature of the crimes and the celebrity status of the victims. Journalists breathlessly printed everything they could find about the murders, and when the facts ran dry, they printed speculation. As a result, much of what they reported in the days following the murders was fantastic and untrue. Some papers said that Sharon Tate's unborn child had been torn from her body or that a towel found across Jay Sebring's face had been a "hood" used in some form of ritual. None of this was true, but it would be a long time before any of it was debunked.

Amazingly, at least one opportunity to link the Hinman murder to the murders at Cielo Drive was missed quite early. During the autopsies for the Cielo Drive victims, a detective from the Los Angeles County Sheriff's Department told an LAPD sergeant about the Hinman killing and how the two crimes bore striking similarities. Both had victims killed with long bladed weapons and messages written nearby in the victims' own blood. One was *Political Piggy* and one was *Pig*. How could these not be connected? The LAPD sergeant waved him off, saying they were convinced that the Cielo Drive murders were somehow drug related. A drug deal gone bad? Some of the victims were known to have been recreational drug users. Maybe one had flipped out and killed the others while on a bad "trip."

What the LAPD did not realize until much later was that they already had a man in custody who was linked to these crimes. Beausoleil had been arrested on August 6, just a couple of days before Tate. He had been arrested while driving Hinman's car, with the murder weapon in the trunk and Hinman's blood on his clothes. He was a known associate of Charles Manson. And law enforcement knew all about Manson and his band of hippies. Still, at the press conference that followed the Tate autopsies, an LAPD detective said, "I don't feel that we have a maniac running around."

The police did make one arrest very quickly in the wake of the Tate murders. Garretson, the caretaker of the Cielo Drive residence, had been arrested when they found him in the house out back. He claimed to have not heard anything during the time the murders occurred, and the police thought he was behaving oddly. News spread that the police had arrested a suspect and media reports made it sound like he was the right person. But he passed a polygraph and was soon released. He was not released, however, until after the LaBiancas had been murdered. To even the most amateurish armchair detectives it was clear: Garretson had nothing to do with either set of killings.

Manson and his Family had been staying at a place called Spahn Ranch, a former western movie set owned by an elderly man named George Spahn. Spahn was half blind, eighty years old, and seemingly only partially aware that

Charles Manson and a couple dozen of his followers were living on the sprawling premises not far from Los Angeles. And, while there, they had been stealing cars and committing other petty crimes, when they weren't out murdering people and trying to start "Helter Skelter." Within a week of the LaBianca murders, police raided the ranch and rounded up Manson and twenty-five others on a warrant for auto theft. After they were all booked, someone noticed that the warrant was misdated. They were all released.

Fearing that Spahn Ranch was not a good place to hide, Manson and the Family moved out to the desert to hide and prepare for the impending apocalypse. As with so many criminals, they did not manage to lay low or stay off the radar of law enforcement. The Family continued stealing cars and dune buggies and police began noticing that stolen vehicles were seen in and around an area known as the Barker Ranch. Law enforcement once again raided the Manson encampment and rounded up twenty-four people, one of whom was Charles Manson.

Manson was famously found hiding in a cabinet under the bathroom sink of a building the Family had been staying in. Even so, the officers arresting him and the others had no idea that the little hippie under the sink was the mastermind of the recent murder spree in Los Angeles. When he was booked, he gave his name as Charles Manson. Asked if he was known by any other names, he told them to list *Jesus Christ* and *God*. At that point in his life, Manson had already spent seventeen years of his life—about half—in jail, prison, or some other kind of penal institution.

The Family members sat in jail awaiting various charges related to weapons and stolen autos and managed to stay quiet for a while. A small break in the case came in the form of Kitty Lutesinger, who was picked up by police near the Barker Ranch. She told police that she was scared of the Manson Family and wanted to escape, but she was pregnant with Bobby Beausoleil's child. She said she did not know where he was—but the police did. He was in jail, having been arrested for the Hinman murder. She gave the police a statement that started connecting up the various crimes to Manson. The rest of the connections would come from Manson Family members talking in jail. One told a cellmate about her involvement in the Hinman murder, and soon the entire chain of events became clear to law enforcement. Warrants were issued for the few Family members not in custody, and the rest were located and rounded up.

Beausoleil was placed on trial for the Hinman murder. In fact, his case was so straightforward that his trial took place before Manson had even been picked up in the Barker Ranch raid. Prosecutors did not realize at first that it was part of a larger picture, involving Manson and his Family. The jury could not reach a verdict, however. Beausoleil was retried, and after Mary Brunner—who had been given immunity for her testimony—described how he had stabbed the music teacher to death, he was convicted and sentenced to death.

During the time leading up to Beausoleil's conviction, the

Cielo Drive and LaBianca murders had been assigned to an experienced prosecuting attorney named Vincent Bugliosi. Bugliosi would examine and investigate the cases and manage to paint a clear picture of the bizarre world of Charles Manson, a world where a little career criminal could persuade hippies to go out and commit brutal murders of strangers in the name of a half-baked cultish philosophy. Bugliosi would prosecute Manson and the rest and eventually write a bestselling book about it.

Manson and three others—Tex Watson successfully fought extradition until after the Manson trial started—were charged and put on trial for the Cielo Drive and LaBianca murders. The trials began on June 15, 1970, and were a convoluted affair. Watson was instrumental in the killings at the Cielo Drive house and the LaBianca home. Eventually, he would be brought to California for trial.

Manson and his co-defendants did everything they could to slow down and disrupt the trial. During one pretrial hearing, he insisted on sitting with his chair backward, facing away from the judge. When the judge threatened him with contempt, he ignored the warning. He was hauled out and placed in a room where he could hear the proceedings through a speaker system. Shortly after, the co-defendants—Susan Atkins, Leslie Van Houten, and Patricia Krenwinkel—all did the same thing. They, too, were sent to a room where they could listen to the trial without disrupting the proceedings. This was a low-key precursor for what was to follow. Manson filed a motion with the court requesting that the court release him forthwith since, as he put it, he was "Jesus Christ-Prisoner." The judge denied the motion. Manson had a sense of humor, according to Bugliosi, as did the judge. At one point, Manson addressed the court:

"Well, I was going to ask him [the district attorney] if he would call the whole thing off. It would save a lot of trouble."

To which the judge responded, "Disappoint all these people? Never, Mr. Manson."

Not all of Manson's Family was on trial, and many of the ones who had escaped being charged with crimes attended court every day. They would mill around outside the courthouse or sit in the gallery and watch. Before the trial started, three of them stood up and began yelling at the judge, who rewarded them with a finding of contempt and five days in jail. Bugliosi served subpoenas on many of them and then asked the court to sequester witnesses before they testified. He had no intention of calling them to the stand—although he could have if he wanted to; the maneuver just made them all stay out of the courtroom during the trial.

More worrisome was that some of the Family members who were not on trial were undoubtedly still under Manson's spell. The judge received around-the-clock protection from the sheriff's department, and the jury was sequestered. While juries are often sequestered to shield them from publicity about the trial while it is in progress, here there was a real concern that Family members might try to harm jurors before the trial ended. During the trial, Family members began menacing Bugliosi, and Manson told a bailiff he was going to have the prosecutor killed; Bugliosi was assigned a bodyguard as well. It degenerated to the point where the defense attorneys were hinting that they, too, had their lives threatened by their own clients.

On the first day of the trial, Manson was brought into court with a bloody X he had carved in his own forehead. His followers—the ones not on trial with him—handed out copies of a typewritten statement Manson had dictated, explaining: "I have X'd myself from your world." The statement rambled on. The following weekend, the co-defendants all similarly carved up their own foreheads and soon, many of the Family members who loitered near the courthouse followed suit. These same Family members often slept in the bushes by the courthouse overnight.

The trial featured daily theatrics. At one point, Manson leaped over the counsel table and tried stabbing the judge with a pencil. After he was tackled by bailiffs he yelled, "In the name of Christian justice, someone should cut your head off!" On another occasion, he smuggled a newspaper into the court room and held it up so the jury could see a headline where Nixon had proclaimed *Manson Guilty*. His co-defendants stood up and started chanting in unison, sometimes in English, sometimes in Latin. At one point, a defense attorney told the court his client didn't wish to testify. His client, and other defendants, jumped up and yelled that they did want to testify. An argument broke out, which showed that the attorney had no control of his client, and he told the court that the defendants were not following the advice of defense counsel. The lawyer failed to show up for court the next day. He was replaced and after the trial ended, his body was found dumped in Ventura County. He had been murdered by Manson followers.

Manson eventually spoke to the court and denied ordering any murders. He blamed everything on music. "Why blame it on me? I didn't write the music." He apparently wanted the jury to believe that Helter Skelter had started, and his actions had been the inevitable beginning of a much larger movement. No one else saw it that way.

The jury returned guilty verdicts on January 25, 1971. The five defendants, including Manson, were sentenced to death. However, California abolished the death penalty before any of them were executed. As a result, they were all sentenced to life in prison. During the trial, the members of the Family who were not directly involved in the murders made publicity by hanging around the courthouse, sitting on the sidewalk, shaving their heads, and talking about how Manson was a misunderstood visionary. A few years later, one of them, Lynette "Squeaky" Fromme, would gain notoriety by trying to assassinate Gerald Ford when he visited California. The story of Manson became even better known after the prose-cutor on the case, Vincent Bugliosi, wrote the book *Helter Skelter* about the murders and the trials. The book sold more than seven million copies and was twice made into a movie by that name. And while Bugliosi did an amazing job unraveling the facts of each of these murders, a certain amount of uncertainty will probably always cloud these stories. Several members of the Manson Family who testified would later recant testimony. Some committed obvious perjury and later promoted different versions of events in attempts to get sympathy, parole, or media attention.

Of the three Manson Family "Helter Skelter" murder houses, Hinman, Tate, and LaBianca, only Hinman and LaBianca remain. The Tate murder house, 10050 Cielo Drive, had a long and illustrious past before it became the site of a mass murder. It had been built in the early 1940s and was home to many celebrities and movie stars. Silent-film star Lillian Gish lived there, as did Cary Grant, Henry Fonda, Mark Lindsay, Olivia Hussey, Terry Melcher, and his mother, Doris Day—all before the Manson Family turned it into a crime scene. After the murders, Rudy Altobelli moved from the guest house back into the home he had been renting out to others, staying there for the next twenty years. When asked about the house by newspeople, he always said that he felt safe in the home. Altobelli eventually sold the property for $1.6 million.

A well-known figure in music named Trent Reznor rented the house shortly after Altobelli moved out and built a recording studio in it that he called the "Pig" studio. Several of his own albums were recorded there, as was Marilyn Manson's *Portrait of an American Family*. In 1993, Reznor moved out of the house, saying he had a hard time handling the "history" of the house. Still, he reportedly took the front door with him and installed it at his new recording studio. It was the same door on which one of the Manson clan had written *Pig* in blood.

In 1994, the owner of the house knocked it down and built a sixteen-thousand-square-foot mansion in its place. He also changed the address from 10050 to 10066 Cielo Drive. There is nothing recognizable about the property today when compared to the configuration of the estate when Altobelli rented it to Polanski. The only thing remaining from that night is the telephone pole Tex Watson climbed to cut the phone line to the house.

The other two homes, Hinman and LaBianca, are still standing. In 2004, the Hinman house was listed for sale with a typical real estate salesperson's flourish. The home is Mediterranean in style and sits on approximately a third of an acre. Two stories tall, it has four bedrooms and two and a half baths. It was 2,600 square feet and had an asking price of $1.025 million. It is unclear why, but the home was simply taken off the market shortly after the listing appeared. From the narrative description, it is clear why a musician might be drawn to the property. A stream flowed through the yard, over a waterfall. There are "meandering rock walkways" and a gazebo. The house had been substantially updated in later years. Interior touches included marble, a gourmet kitchen, "many pairs of French doors," and "numerous skylights."

In 2012, it was listed for sale again. The asking price had been reduced to $949,000. The home is privately owned. It can be seen from the road, but there is extensive foliage that grants the home a good bit of privacy.

The LaBianca house was 3301 Waverly Drive, in the Los Feliz neighborhood of Los Angeles, south of Griffith Park. At one time, the home was called "Oak Terrace" by its owners. Leno's father, Antonio LaBianca, had bought the house in 1940. Antonio was the founder of Gateway Markets and Leno was his only son. In 1968, Leno LaBianca purchased the Waverly home from his mother. Leno was married at that time to Rosemary, his second wife, and they moved into the home.

In the years following the murders, the home has been modified a bit but is still recognizable. The driveway that climbs to the house from Waverly has been gated and much of the front yard has been turned into a parking area, a portion of which is covered. The house also has a separate garage out back and a swimming pool on its eastern side. The street number has been changed to 3311 Waverly. The house is 1,655 square feet with two bedrooms and two bathrooms and sits on almost three quarters of an acre. It was built in 1922. In 1998, the home sold for $375,000 and by 2012, some sources suggested the house would sell for a little over $800,000 if it were put up for sale. It is privately owned but can be seen from the street.

---

* Vincent Bugliosi and Curt Gentry, *Helter Skelter* (1974).
* Ed Sanders, *The Family* (2002).

The Murder House Where the Mass Murderer Was Killed

DEAN "THE CANDYMAN" CORLL

1973

2020 Lamar Drive
Pasadena, Texas 77502

On August 8, 1973, Elmer Wayne Henley called the police and told them, "Y'all better come here right now. I just killed a man." The police soon arrived at 2020 Lamar Drive and found three teenagers in the front yard: Henley, along with another young man and a teenage girl. When they entered the house, the police found the bullet-riddled naked body of Dean Arnold Corll, the owner of the home. Searching further, they found that the bedroom of the house had been set up as a torture chamber. The floor was covered with plastic and there was a torture board: a sheet of plywood with handcuffs and cables attached to it that was clearly designed to restrain a person. Elsewhere in the room they found more items that made it clear that whoever had outfitted the room had planned on torturing and killing someone there. But who was it?

Dean Arnold Corll was an electrician, but at one time he had been vice president of a family-owned candy company near Houston, Texas. His mother had started the company and it became successful. In 1965, the company was relocated directly across the street from an elementary school. Corll worked at the company and often gave out free candy to schoolchildren, particularly young boys, and was soon nicknamed "The Candyman." Corll had spent time in the military and was now in his late twenties. Even so, he seemed to spend an inordinate amount of time around male children. He hired teenagers and had a pool table in the back of his warehouse, where he encouraged the schoolchildren to hang out with him. And from time to time, schoolchildren from Houston would disappear. In a three-year period in the early 1970s, twenty-eight boys would disappear. This mass murder spree would be the worst of its kind for quite some time and would all come to light on August 8, 1973. Until then, though, very few people even suspected there was anything untoward about Dean Corll, the generous man who gave candy to strangers.

In May 1971, two boys, aged thirteen and sixteen, disappeared from near where Corll lived. When their parents reported them missing to the police, they were told that the children had probably simply run away from home. The police would not look for them unless there was evidence of foul play. Private investigators were hired and flyers were posted, but the children were never seen again. The trend of "runaways" in the area continued. Oddly, none of the runaways ever turned up anywhere. Still, the police seemed unconcerned.

A boy named Frank Aguirre disappeared in early 1972, baffling his family and his girlfriend, Rhonda Williams. Afterward, a boy she knew named Wayne Henley told her that Aguirre had gotten mixed up with some very bad people, organized crime, and would not be returning. He told her that he couldn't tell her anything more because his own life was in danger. As more young boys from the neighborhood disappeared, parents began doing their own investigations. Some of them found out that Dean Corll had some sort of connection to the story. Some of the boys had spent time at Corll's house, listening to music and watching television. The kids had also been given alcohol and drugs by Corll, but the children never would have told their parents that. One mother asked her son point-blank about the activities at Corll's house and was shocked to hear that her son had seen Corll handcuff another boy and then not be able to undo the cuffs because he had "lost" the keys. Corll was questioned by parents but handled the situation coolly. He was polite and respectful.

Corll, Henley, and another teenager named David Brooks had worked as a team. Corll told the other boys he would pay them a bounty for each teenage boy they could procure for him. Working alone and sometimes together, the boys would find targets and promise them alcohol or drugs, which could be found at a party at Corll's place. Corll used several different apartments and sometimes the house on Lamar, which had been owned by his father. Amazingly, the two teenage accomplices often targeted neighborhood friends and former classmates, boys they had known for years. The boys would go to Corll's place for a "party." There, they would be plied with alcohol and drugs and then Corll would overpower them. He would tie them up and often affix them to his torture board, a sheet of plywood to which he had attached handcuffs and cables. Once disabled, the victims would be raped, tortured, and killed. Corll's victims were shot, beaten, strangled, or even kicked to death.

As Corll killed more children, he became increasingly more violent and unpredictable. It was this change in his behavior that frightened Henley to the point where he would shoot Corll. On August 7, 1973, Henley planned on going back to Corll's place with a boy named Tim Kerley. If Corll made Kerley a victim, Henley would collect his fee from Corll. But Rhonda Williams lived nearby, and she had told Henley that she had been having problems with her alcoholic father. Henley said he would come by and take her someplace where she could spend the night. He brought her to Corll's place. Corll was not happy that Henley had brought a female to his house and became angry with Henley. Corll let the teens drink and do drugs, though, as if all were forgiven. As the next day approached, the teens either fell asleep or became intoxicated.

Henley awoke to find himself bound, with handcuffs on his wrists. Kerley was naked, strapped to the torture board, and Williams was restrained as well.

Corll spoke with Henley and told him that his only choice was to rape Williams while Corll would rape Kerley. Henley told Corll he would, and Corll undid his handcuffs. Kerley and Williams were now both awake and in shock. Williams asked Henley, "Is this for real?" When he said it was, she asked, "Are you going to do anything about it?"

Henley found a gun that Corll owned and shot Corll with it. Corll staggered from the room while Henley shot him a few more times. As Corll died in the hallway, Henley released Kerley and Williams. Henley then called the police and the three went and sat in front of the house, waiting for them to arrive.

At first, the police were unsure of what to make of the story told them by the three. Henley was claiming he killed Corll in self-defense, but it was clear that Henley was also involved on some level. Could he have simply made up the whole story? Perhaps Corll was a victim? Henley began telling them everything he knew about Corll. Perhaps they should start with the boat shed. Henley told the police that Corll took the bodies of his victims to a couple of places he had found where he could dispose of bodies discreetly. One place was a boat storage facility where the sheds had dirt floors. Corll buried the bodies under the shed floor after covering them with lime. When Henley brought the police to the shed, they unearthed seventeen bodies.

He then took them to a few other places he knew of where more bodies were recovered.

As police unraveled the story of the missing boys, it became clear that Henley and Brooks were also culpable. The two were tried for murder. Henley received six life terms for his role in the deaths of six boys. Brooks was found guilty of one murder and also received a life term.

The house on Lamar Drive had been owned by Corll's father and was built in 1952. It was small, with only a little over 1,200 square feet of living space on a 7,000-square-foot lot. It last sold in a traditional transaction in 1999. It suffered a bank foreclosure in 2001 and its foreclosure price was reported to be $56,123.

Real Murders
in a Fake Haunted House

THE AMITYVILLE HORROR HOUSE

1974

108 Ocean Avenue (formerly 112 Ocean Avenue)
Amityville, New York 11701

Ronald DeFeo and his wife, Louise, lived in a large house in Amityville, New York. They had five children, the oldest of whom was Ronald Jr., known as "Butch." On November 14, 1974, around 3:00 A.M., twenty-three-year-old Butch took a hunting rifle and crept into his parents' bedroom. He shot his father twice and quickly shot his mother twice as well. They would each die rather quickly. Butch then went to the room shared by his two brothers. He shot each of them once, killing them both. He then went to the bedroom shared by his sisters and shot each of them in the head as they lay sleeping. He had managed to kill all six family members without waking them, and the neighbors did not hear any of the gunfire. Butch showered and dressed for work. He drove into Brooklyn and disposed of the gun and the clothes he had been wearing by throwing them down a storm drain. He then went to work and acted as if nothing had happened. After he returned home from work, he ran into a local bar and called out for help, saying, "You got to help me! I think my mother and father are shot." Soon thereafter, the police were called to the scene and confirmed that six people were dead. The horrific murders in Amityville would soon be overshadowed by a fictional account of what supposedly happened in the house after Butch DeFeo's murder spree.

Amityville is one of those names that has taken on a secondary meaning very different from the original. Most Americans, hearing the name of the village in New York State, immediately think of the 1979 film *The Amityville Horror*, starring James Brolin, Margot Kidder, and Rod Steiger. The movie was based on a bestselling 1977 book of the same name by Jay Anson, which told the story of the Lutz family, driven out of a haunted house. The book's subtitle claimed it was *A True Story*. Much of the story is actually fiction, but the house is real.

While the killing of six family members is a horrific event, the DeFeo murders would be elevated to something different altogether. The slayings would be the genesis of a ghostly controversy swirling around the house at 112 Ocean Avenue, which the DeFeos had bought in 1965. Ronald DeFeo Sr. sold Buicks for a living. He and his wife, Louise, had five children: two daughters, Dawn and Allison, and three sons, Ronald Jr., Marc, and John Matthew.

Ronald Sr. gave Butch a cushy job at his car dealership, one where he got paid even when he didn't show up for work. The other workers didn't mind when Butch skipped work, though, because he didn't accomplish much when he was there. Over time, Butch's relationship with his father deteriorated. The two argued, and one night Butch leveled a loaded shotgun at Ronald Sr. while trying to make a point. Ronald believed that Butch was not only lazy but also a thief. Their biggest fight started when Butch stole more than $20,000 from the dealership, money he was supposed to deposit at the bank. Butch took the money and told people he had been robbed but no one believed him. Butch used the money he stole to buy drugs. Shortly after that, Ronald Sr. and Butch had another ugly argument; the exchange ended with Butch yelling at his father, "You fat prick, I'll kill you."

Butch told the police he was afraid the murders were a mob hit, and he even gave them the name of a man he believed might have been the killer. Soon, however, Butch's story fell apart. The "mobster's" alibi checked out. Worse for Butch, the gun he had used to shoot his family was a .35-caliber Marlin hunting rifle and although he had thrown it away, its box was still in his bedroom when the police searched the house.

Forensic experts had identified the murder weapon as a fairly uncommon .35-caliber hunting rifle. Eventually, Butch admitted he killed his family.

On October 14, 1975, Butch's trial began. The prosecution noted that Butch was a user of LSD and heroin but argued that he understood his actions when he killed his family. He certainly wasn't insane. After the killings, he had not only confessed but also led the police to the murder weapon, which was positively linked to the crimes.

The defense, not having much to work with in the face of such overwhelming evidence, pleaded not guilty by reason of insanity. When he took the stand in his own defense, DeFeo attempted to convince the jury that he was, indeed, insane by acting insane on the witness stand. DeFeo claimed that he had heard the victims' voices in his head, plotting against him. His attorney held up a photograph of DeFeo's mother—whom he had shot and killed as she lay in bed—and asked DeFeo to identify her for the jury. He angrily responded, "I told you before and I'll say it again. I never saw this person before in my life. I don't know who this person is." When shown a photograph of his father he answered, "Did I kill him? I killed them all. Yes, sir. I killed them all in self-defense." Later, he testified, "I am God."

The jury didn't buy any of it, finding him guilty on six counts of second-degree murder. He was sentenced to six concurrent sentences of twenty-five years to life. Although the mass murder made headlines at the time, it probably would have faded from memory if an imaginative couple hadn't bought the former DeFeo house shortly after.

A little over a year after the murders, new owners moved into the DeFeo house, having paid $80,000 for it. On December 18, 1975, the Lutz family began what would be a short but infamous stay in the house. George Lutz, his wife, Kathleen, and three children had been told by their real estate agent of the DeFeo murders but had decided to purchase the house anyway. Just twenty-eight days after moving in, the Lutzes vacated the house.

They claimed they had been driven out by all manner of paranormal activity that had taken place in the house. They said the walls oozed a mysterious slime, voices told them to get out, and huge swarms of insects materialized out of nowhere, in the dead of winter. A ghostly pig with glowing eyes appeared and talked to one of their children. They named the pig "Jodie." A priest who had come to bless the house at the move-in later supposedly told the Lutzes that he had been warned by a voice to get out of the house but hadn't bothered to tell them about it.

It was January 14, 1976, when the Lutzes fled the house and sent movers back to retrieve their furniture. In March 1977, Jim and Barbara Cromarty bought the house from the Lutzes for $55,000 and moved in. They experienced no paranormal activity and said that they found no evidence of slime, ghostly pigs with glow-in-the-dark eyes, or any of the damage the Lutzes had claimed had been caused by supernatural entities.

A writer named Jay Anson met the Lutzes and agreed to write a book about their experience in the DeFeo murder house. In September 1977, *The Amityville Horror: A True Story* was published. The book recounted the bizarre story of the Lutzes being driven from the DeFeo house. The book went on to sell more than ten million copies and was twice adapted for films that spawned numerous sequels. Dozens of books and television shows have been based on some aspect of the story.

The book that started it all, *The Amityville Horror: A True Story*, listed the Lutzes as co-authors. Its introduction also stated that the Lutzes had "cut off all communication with the media, feeling that too much was being overstated and exaggerated." Of course, the book thrust the Lutzes into the spotlight in a manner unlike anything that had happened to them before the book was published, and they were soon doing the talk show circuit, telling interviewers about their brush with ghosts and supernatural slime. It is hard to imagine any part of their story being more overstated or exaggerated than their own telling of it.

In later years, various skeptics would comb through the book and note many discrepancies between the story and the known facts or events that could be double-checked. For example, the Lutzes claimed to have called the police during their hauntings; the police had no records of any calls. The priest who was said to have witnessed evil doings at the house denied having seen any such thing. He said he had never heard the voice telling him to "get out!" and he had never told the Lutzes that he had. And to cap it off, William Weber, the attorney who had represented Butch DeFeo in his murder trial, told *People* magazine that the entire story was a fabrication. "I know this book's a hoax. We created this horror story over many bottles of wine." Weber said he had introduced the Lutzes to the writer who would turn their story into a best-seller. There are still believers out there, some of whom are convinced that Weber is only disavowing the story because he wasn't cut in on the profits from the story. There is at least one book debunking the story: *The Amityville Horror Conspiracy*, by Stephen Kaplan.

Meanwhile, the Cromartys—who had bought the house from the Lutzes—had to deal with the attention paid to the house by people who had read the book or seen the movie. "Nothing weird ever happened, except for people coming by because of the book and the movie," James Cromarty later said. After living in the house for a decade, the Cromartys sold the house to Peter and Jeanne O'Neill, who also lived in the house for ten years. Jeanne said, "I loved it. It was a beautiful home." When the O'Neills sold it in 1997, they got $310,000 for it.

What confuses some visitors to the house is that it does not look like the one in the film. *The Amityville Horror* film-makers used a house a hundred miles away in Toms River,

New Jersey, to shoot their film, and that house has its own problems. The house sits at 100 Terrace Avenue, at the corner of Terrace and Lowell. In 2012, its owner was renting it and the tenants claimed the house was haunted. They sued their landlord to break the lease, and the landlord filed a counter-suit against the tenants. He argued that unfounded "haunted house" claims amounted to defamation and would devalue the property. The renters appeared on *Good Morning America* to explain how the house that played the role of a haunted house in a movie was, itself, also haunted now. The producers of *The People's Court* offered to let the litigants appear on their show to settle the dispute in the most appropriate fashion: in front of a television audience. The parties agreed to appear. After hearing evidence that included tape recordings made by the tenants, the court ruled in favor of the landlord. The house that played the role of the Amityville Horror house in the movies was not actually haunted and the tenants had to pay their rent.

Regardless of the Lutz claims, the Amityville house once owned by the DeFeo family was the site of a gruesome mass murder. The DeFeo house is described as Dutch Colonial revival and was built in 1927. It has five bedrooms, three and a half baths, and a detached garage. It is about 3,600 square feet and sits sideways on a quarter-acre lot with one boundary being the Amityville River. The address has been changed in an attempt to discourage people from looking for the house.

Major portions of the exterior of the house have also been remodeled. In 2010, it was reportedly sold for $950,000. A recent property listing called the house "legendary" but did not mention its murderous past. The house is privately owned.

---

* Steven R. Weisman, "Accused in Family's Murder, DeFeo Implicated in $19,000 Theft," *New York Times*, November 17, 1974.

America's Worst
Family Mass Murderer

JAMES RUPPERT

1975

635 Minor Avenue
Hamilton, Ohio 45015

On Easter Sunday, 1975, forty-one-year-old James Ruppert was hungover and still in bed when his brother, sister-in-law, and their eight children arrived at the tiny house he shared with his mother, Charity, in Hamilton, Ohio. James and his brother were polar opposites; while James was unemployed and a loner, his older brother, Leonard, had a career and a large, happy family. When the children came in for lunch, James dragged himself out of bed. Seeming unaware of the holiday festivities, James told his brother he was going to do a little target shooting and brought out three handguns and a rifle.

James Ruppert's vehicle at the time was an old Volkswagen and he had recently been having engine problems with it.

While many people would have thought the difficulties resulted from a lack of maintenance on an old vehicle, James had told a psychiatrist that he believed his older brother had been secretly sabotaging the vehicle when he wasn't around. He couldn't prove it and he had never seen Leonard harming the car, but he was certain of it. James Ruppert blamed his brother for most of the problems he encountered in his life. When Ruppert came into the kitchen, his brother Leonard asked him about the VW, "How's your Volkswagen, Jimmie?"

James Ruppert snapped. He responded to the question by shooting his brother. He then shot his mother and sister-in-law. He shot a nephew and two nieces in the kitchen as well, before going into the living room and shooting the other five children, a niece and four nephews. All eleven died of gunshot wounds. The children ranged in age from four to seventeen.

The shooting lasted only five minutes. In all, Ruppert fired more than thirty shots. He then changed his clothing and stayed in the house for three hours before calling the police. "There's been a shooting here," he was reported to have said. When asked to clarify he simply said, "There are bodies in the house." He then went and sat by the front door, waiting for police officers to arrive.

Ruppert's brief spree was the worst American mass murder to involve a single family. At barely one thousand square feet, Charity's house is perhaps the smallest to make the list of infamous American murder houses. The cramped quarters may have even fueled some of the friction between mother and son.

James Ruppert was born in 1934 and had a troubled life. His father died when he was twelve and he had an older brother with whom he always felt competitive. While his brother, Leonard, found a good job working at General Electric, Ruppert never attained success. He briefly studied drafting in college but dropped out after struggling with grades. He also had trouble with women. Meanwhile, Leonard married Ruppert's ex-girlfriend and fathered eight children, certainly another source of the resentment he felt toward him.

Ruppert had trouble keeping jobs and drank to excess. When unemployed, he divided his time between his mother's house and local bars. Ruppert's behavior began to get more eccentric over time. In 1965, a woman who worked at the local library called the police regarding a threatening phone call she had received. She recognized the caller as Ruppert because he often spent time at the library. When the police questioned him, Ruppert admitted he had made the call. The police already knew of Ruppert. He had a collection of guns and was often down at the local river, firing them off. He hadn't hurt anyone or broken any laws yet, however. He had merely appeared on their radar, so to speak. With respect to the incident with the phone call to the library worker, law enforcement suggested he seek mental help but declined to prosecute him.

During his questioning after the library incident, Ruppert had told the police he believed he was being watched by the

FBI and that his mother and brother were somehow in league with the authorities. To the police, Ruppert appeared paranoid but not terribly dangerous. Hamilton was home to more than sixty thousand people and the police had more important crimes to deal with than prank phone calls. Ruppert was seen by psychiatrists. He told them that he was being followed by the police. Local, county, state, they were all involved in watching him, he told the doctor. They were following him and keeping tabs on him, just like the FBI. The psychiatrists continued talking to him but also concluded that he was not a threat. He was not hospitalized or medicated. It seems that Ruppert was one of those people that everyone thought was a little nuts. But was he dangerous?

In 1975, his mother finally had enough. She had been charging him rent to stay in the home and he had fallen behind in his payments. She told James she was going to kick him out of the house unless he got caught up on the rent. Unemployed and already in debt to his brother, a depressed Ruppert saw no way to come up with the money his mother wanted. He went to a local gun dealer and asked about buying a gun silencer. The man told him that they were illegal and Ruppert would have to go elsewhere to find one. Ruppert then went down to a local river and engaged in one of his favorite pastimes, a little target practice with one of his handguns. Several people saw him firing his .357 at the river's edge on that Easter weekend. That Saturday was Ruppert's forty-first birthday.

Ruppert spent the evening of his birthday drinking at a

local bar and complaining about life to anyone who would listen. The bartender was a woman Ruppert often spoke to, one of few women he had much interaction with. While drinking, Ruppert said something about having a problem that needed to be "taken care of." He mentioned his mother threatening to evict him and then he left. He came back a little while later and the bartender asked him if he had just taken care of his problem. Ruppert told her, "No, not yet." He continued drinking there until the bar closed. The next day was when he killed his entire family.

When the police arrived at the house with the eleven murder victims, Ruppert was cooperative and calm. Investigators inspected the scene and were shocked. Each victim had been shot twice: once through the body and then a "kill" shot through the head or heart. The police chief, prosecutor, and coroner all surveyed the scene. There was so much blood that one investigator later said that he had to be careful not to let it drip on him as he walked through the basement; the blood was seeping through the floorboards.

The police chief told the press: "This kind of murder usually has as its motive something like sex, or greed, or jealousy. We can find none of those things here." Upon viewing the facts of the case, most people eventually came to believe that jealousy was a factor, jealousy felt by a man with mental problems.

Although he had called the police and made no effort to run, Ruppert was not cooperative with the prosecution once charges were filed. He faced eleven counts of murder; his defense attorneys claimed he was insane. He awaited trial, held on a $200,000 bond. The prosecution presented the theory that Ruppert was not insane; they said he had planned the killings and turned himself in to the police specifically so he could plead insanity. Since the entire family was dead, Ruppert stood to inherit from the estates of his mother, his brother, and even the nieces and nephews. And, under Ohio law, he could inherit all of that and $300,000 of life insurance proceeds if he was found not guilty by reason of insanity. Ruppert's financial problems would finally be solved if he could pull it off. The prosecutors would pitch this theory to the jury: Ruppert's motive was financial, pure and simple.

Under Ohio law, Ruppert had the choice of facing a jury or a panel of three judges. While a jury had to rule unanimously, it would take only two of the three judges to vote and reach a verdict. The judges still seemed like a safer bet on a case so sure to be emotionally charged. After all, he had killed eight children, one of whom was only four years old. He opted for the judges. Three Butler County Common Pleas judges heard the evidence and arguments regarding Ruppert's shooting rampage. His trial ended on July 3, 1975, when two of the three judges ruled that he was guilty of all eleven counts of aggravated murder and sentenced him to eleven consecutive terms of life in prison.

Ruppert appealed his conviction. His attorneys argued that the trial court had misled Ruppert and his trial counsel. They claimed they were told that the panel of judges would only be able to convict Ruppert with a unanimous verdict, the same way a jury of twelve would have worked. Ruppert said that if he had known that they could convict him with a split vote, he would have asked for a jury trial. The Ohio Supreme Court said that if it was true that he'd been misled, Ruppert was entitled to a new trial. The prosecutors appealed the ruling to the U.S. Supreme Court, which declined to overturn the state court. While appealing his conviction, Ruppert had been held at the Lima State Hospital for the criminally insane. His attorney told reporters in 1978, shortly after the Supreme Court had refused to rule on the case—which was, for his purposes, the same as winning—that he didn't even believe Ruppert was competent to stand trial. "His paranoid condition has worsened. Generally, his entire mental processes are breaking down."

A second trial was ordered and the venue was changed to Findlay, Ohio, for fear that an unbiased jury could not be found in Hamilton. Again, he was deemed competent to stand trial, and he was again found guilty on July 23, 1982. This time he was found guilty on two counts—for the murder of his mother and brother—but found not guilty by reason of insanity for the other nine killings. Many people took the verdict to mean that Ruppert knew what he was doing when he killed his brother and mother but may have then continued the killing in some sort of blind rage. He was sentenced to two consecutive life sentences. He is not eligible for a parole hearing until 2035—the year he would turn 101 years old.

The house where James Ruppert killed eleven people is quite small. It must have seemed cramped even when just James and his mother were home. It is only 1,076 square feet, with two bedrooms and one bathroom. It was built in 1919 and the lot it occupies is just under 3,800 square feet. In 2008, it sold for $54,000. It still stands and is privately owned.

---

* "Officials Puzzled by Mass Murder," *Lawrence (KS) Journal-World*, April 1, 1975.

The Unicorn Murder

IRA EINHORN

1977

3411 Race Street
Philadelphia, Pennsylvania 19104

Helen "Holly" Maddux was a peace-loving thirty-year-old woman, a former prep school cheerleader who would never hurt anyone. She was living with Ira Einhorn, a well-known Philadelphian and proponent of world peace and Earth Day. A newspaper reporter from Philadelphia named Ronnie Polaneczky called him "a counterculture icon of the '60s and '70s[;] he was a hippie guru to the rich, famous and influential, mesmerizing them with messages of peace, love, intellectual enlightenment and global connectivity." Among his friends and followers were rock stars, CEOs of huge corporations, and even politicians. One aspect of his character that added to his mystique was his claim that dark forces in the government were out to get him. It is unclear why that would have been, since most people saw his philosophy as little more than that of an old-school hippie who hadn't changed with the times. His name—Einhorn—translated from German means "one horn." He often called himself the Unicorn.

After a few years of sharing the apartment in Philadelphia, Holly broke up with Einhorn and moved out. She moved to New York City and called Einhorn to tell him she was starting over and wanted to make arrangements to retrieve her belongings. According to prosecutors who conducted two trials, Einhorn was furious. They say he told her he was going to take what she had left behind and throw it away unless she came and picked it up immediately. She went back to Philadelphia to get her things and no one ever heard from her again. It was September 1977.

Later, prosecutors argued that Einhorn—a huge man—beat the diminutive Holly in the apartment. They did not know if he used a weapon or simply slammed her around, but her skull was crushed with half a dozen fractures. As she was dying, she was stuffed into a steamer trunk, her body was covered with newspapers and old shopping bags, and the trunk was shoved into a closet. Prosecutors said that Einhorn padlocked the closet and went on with his life. When people asked about Holly, he told them that she had simply gone to the store one day and never came back. After all, she had been threatening to leave him. All the while, over almost two years,

Holly's body was in the trunk in the closet, in the apartment Einhorn continued to occupy.

After Holly's disappearance, the police investigated and even questioned Einhorn. He told them the same story: She had gone to the store and never returned. He had assumed she had finally left him, something she had been threatening to do often, he told them. With nothing else to go on, the police went and looked elsewhere. They had not searched the apartment.

The Maddux family grew frustrated at the lack of progress being made by the police and hired private detectives to look for their daughter. The detectives found witnesses who told them that in the days after Holly vanished, Einhorn had sought help in disposing of a trunk that was too heavy for him to move by himself from his apartment. He claimed it held top-secret documents. The friends did not help him move the trunk and said that as far as they knew, the trunk was still in Einhorn's apartment.

A little more checking by the detectives—and the police, who were now curious about the secret-document trunk—revealed that Einhorn's neighbors may also have had something to contribute to the investigation. There was a foul odor coming from Einhorn's apartment that was so bad that the building supervisor had tried to intervene. When he called on Einhorn to see about it, Einhorn had refused to let him into the apartment. Worse, the neighbor who lived directly below

Einhorn had discovered that his ceiling—directly below Einhorn's closet floor—had a putrid liquid seeping through it. It resisted cleaning and fresh paint wouldn't fix it. The police sought a search warrant.

It was March 1979 when the police searched Einhorn's apartment. They immediately noticed the locked closet, but Einhorn told them that he had lost the key and pretended that nothing was amiss. As they searched the apartment, detectives broke the lock off a closet and opened the door. Inside the closet they found Holly's belongings, including her purse, her luggage, and her ID. She had obviously not gone anywhere or "left" Einhorn. There was a large trunk in the closet, the obvious source of the smell and the fluid that had been seeping into the apartment below. The detectives opened it and found Holly's body inside, under a layer of old newspapers and shopping bags.

Einhorn stood to the side and watched it all calmly. When a detective said to him that it looked like Holly, Einhorn famously responded, "You found what you found." Einhorn was arrested. Detectives photographed everything they could find in the apartment and gathered evidence. Among items they found were numerous journals Einhorn had kept, diaries that detailed many of his personal relationships.

Despite the apparently overwhelming evidence against him, Einhorn was granted bail. Einhorn had many wealthy benefactors and managed to hire one of the most famous attorneys in Pennsylvania: Arlen Specter. Specter would become a senator in 1980 but first found fame as a member of the Warren Commission. There, as a young attorney, he had been the one who postulated the "single bullet theory" to explain the various bullet wounds to John F. Kennedy and John Connally. For Einhorn, he worked a miracle. Specter talked the judge into releasing Einhorn on bond, despite the fact that he was facing a murder charge. The judge allowed a ridiculously low bond of $40,000—and then made Einhorn post just ten percent of it. It meant that $4,000 was all it took for Einhorn to walk out of court a free man before his trial. The money was posted by one of his many supporters, apparently convinced that the peaceful Unicorn could not possibly have had anything to do with the rotting dead body in the closet in his apartment.

Shortly before his trial, Einhorn vanished. He fled the country and went to Ireland, where he began a new life with a new name. He then spent the next few years eluding the authorities, running from one country to the next—England, Sweden, France; all the while he had supporters who sent him money, believing in his innocence. He would later brag that while he was on the run, he spent time with rock stars and rich people, often just sitting and discussing his philosophies and how they believed him when he told them that the U.S. government was trying to frame him for murder.

While Einhorn was absent from the United States, the prosecution had decided to try him for murder. Since he had been notified of the trial and ordered to appear, the court could legally proceed and try him in absentia. It is an uncommon occurrence but perfectly legal under Pennsylvania law. Einhorn could have appeared and defended himself if he wanted to; he clearly chose not to. The jury heard the evidence and found Einhorn guilty of murder in 1993.

Einhorn managed to evade capture until 1997. A prosecutor in Philadelphia had dedicated himself to bringing Einhorn to justice and spent decades studying Einhorn's life and a stack of journals he had left behind. After several near-misses, he found out about a woman in Sweden who seemed to have some connection to Einhorn. When questioned, she feigned ignorance. Then she disappeared. The prosecutor asked international law enforcement to look for her, and they found that she had recently applied for a French driver's license. Some more legwork revealed that she had moved to France and married a man whose name was an alias Einhorn had used previously.

The police tracked the couple to a farmhouse in a small village in France, where they found Einhorn. He had married the wealthy Swedish woman and the two had started a new life together in a place *Time* magazine likened to living in an "Impressionist painting." Einhorn first told the police they had the wrong man, but it was to no avail. They took him into custody. Even so, it would be a while before the Unicorn was returned to America.

Einhorn's luck continued. Coupled with his ability to use

the legal process to his advantage, he managed to foil the efforts of the Americans who wanted to bring him back to America. Once again, Einhorn hired the best attorneys money could buy. When the U.S. sought to extradite Einhorn, his attorneys in France noted two irregularities in the proceedings, at least from the French perspective. International law does not favor verdicts resulting from trials conducted with a defendant in absentia, even when the defendant fled the country to avoid the trial. And Pennsylvania had the death penalty. Einhorn's legal team told the authorities in France that Einhorn had been sentenced to death. This caused a stir in a country with no death penalty. Eventually, officials from the United States convinced the French authorities that Einhorn had been given a life sentence and could not, at this point, be sentenced to death. His attorneys then made a convoluted argument: Although he had been sentenced to life in prison at the first trial, what if prosecutors sought the death penalty in a retrial? The French government would not extradite Einhorn if he faced even the possibility of the death penalty in the United States. Einhorn would use these arguments to delay his extradition. After six months in a French prison while these arguments were being hashed out, Einhorn was set free.

Time magazine noted that Einhorn had managed to end up in a rather unusual circumstance. As long as he stayed in France, he would be a free man despite having been convicted of murder in the United States. In essence, he had been sentenced to "life in the south of France."

The only solution was a diplomatic one: The State of Pennsylvania had to agree to let Einhorn have another trial. To do this, the state legislature had to pass an actual law for this purpose alone. And they had to agree to not seek the death penalty in the new trial. None of this had anything to do with the merits of the case. It was simply to appease the French government so they would release a convicted murderer who had sought refuge in their country.

The French government did not agree to ship Einhorn back with the new law's passage, however. They simply agreed to hold an extradition hearing for him. Einhorn was arrested again, but amazingly, the French let him post bail. Oddly, Einhorn did not flee this time. On May 27, 1999, Einhorn lost his first extradition hearing. In 2000, he lost an appeal. The European Court on Human Rights also denied to hear his case in 2001. In July of that year, Einhorn was returned to the United States to face a retrial for the murder of Holly Maddux.

In 2002, Einhorn went on trial, but not before his attorneys trotted out every argument they could think of. They argued that the "Einhorn Law" that had been passed to grant the new trial was a conflict between branches of the government. What right did the legislature have to overrule a court's verdict? The argument went up on appeal but the higher courts let the new law stand, clearing the way for the second trial. Then his attorneys tried arguing that Einhorn's second trial violated his double jeopardy rights—that is, he would be tried twice for the same crime. It was a bizarre argument:

Most defendants would make the argument about the second trial because they'd rather have the outcome of the first. Here, Einhorn had been found guilty of murder the first time and sentenced to life in prison. Einhorn's arguments here failed as well. He would stand trial.

At trial, the prosecution argued that Einhorn was violent and had killed Maddux when she had tried leaving him. Einhorn argued that the CIA or other mysterious forces had framed him because he knew too much about top-secret mind-control experiments. Einhorn took the stand, an occasion the prosecutor appeared to enjoy. It allowed him to ask Einhorn to read passages from his diaries to the jury. "To kill what you love seems so natural that strangling Rita last night seemed so right." The "Rita" in that particular passage was—according to the prosecution—Rita Resnick, a woman whom Einhorn had tried strangling shortly before Einhorn wrote the passage. Elsewhere in the same journals he had written, "Sadism—sounds nice—run it over your tongue—contemplate with joy the pains of others." And, "To beat a woman—what joy."

The jury did not buy the CIA frame-up defense. Apparently, the jury found it hard to believe that Einhorn spent almost two years in his apartment with the victim's body in his closet and didn't know it—even as other people in the building complained about something being amiss in the apartment. The jury found Einhorn guilty of first-degree murder. They deliberated for less than three hours. He was sentenced to life in prison without the possibility of parole.

The building where Einhorn killed Holly Maddux still stands on Race Street in Philadelphia, in a neighborhood known as Powelton Village. The building itself was first constructed in the early 1870s—dates given range from 1870 to 1875—and has undergone some modification in the ensuing years. It was first built as a two-story structure, and a third story was added somewhere along the way. It is in a style called Second Empire, which, although ancient-sounding today, was not all that old when the building first went up. A large two-story porch was also added to the building at one time but was later sealed in. There are eleven rental units in the building. Recent listings show them priced in the $1,500-a-month range.

For what it's worth, Einhorn wrote a book titled *Prelude to Intimacy.* In its foreword he wrote, "I did NOT kill Holly Maddux."

---

* Dave Lindorff, "For Ira Einhorn, a Fate Worse Than Death," *Salon*, October 18, 2002.

* "Ronnie Polaneczky: The Ira Einhorn Interview," *(Philadelphia) Daily News*, October 14, 2010.

* Steve Lopez, "The Search for the Unicorn," *Time*, September 29, 1997.

The Murder of John Lennon

THE DAKOTA

1980

1 West 72nd Street
New York, New York 10023

On December 8, 1980, a mentally ill twenty-five-year-old man from Hawaii walked into a bookstore in New York City and bought a copy of *The Catcher in the Rye*. He had read the book previously and was obsessed with it. He wrote *This is my statement* inside the front cover and then put *Holden Caulfield* below that, as if it were his signature. It wasn't; his real name was Mark David Chapman. Chapman then walked over to a large co-op apartment building named the Dakota. The Dakota was one of the most expensive and well-known co-ops in New York City. It faced Central Park and units in it cost millions of dollars. It housed some of New York City's richest and most famous residents.

Chapman lingered near the front entrance of the Dakota. Along with the book *The Catcher in the Rye,* he also had a copy of the LP record *Double Fantasy.* John Lennon and Yoko Ono owned five apartments in the Dakota and lived there with their young son. Lennon actually walked past Chapman into the building at one point when Chapman did not see him. A little later, the housekeeper took Sean, Ono and Lennon's son, for a walk and Chapman recognized the child as Lennon's. He approached the two and tried shaking the young boy's hand.

In the early evening, Lennon and Ono walked out the front door of the Dakota and as they walked toward a limo, Chapman approached Lennon and asked him if he would autograph the record he had brought. Lennon obliged. A photographer on the street caught the moment on film, Lennon signing the album cover with Chapman looking on. Lennon and Ono then left. Chapman stayed, lurking near the entrance of the building.

Almost six hours later, shortly before 11:00 P.M., Lennon and Ono returned to the Dakota, and their limo let them out at the curb. The two walked toward the entrance. Chapman was still there. As Lennon walked through the door to the building, Chapman pulled out a .38-caliber handgun and fired it five times at Lennon, hitting him four times. Lennon stumbled into the building, entering the office of the doorman. Yoko screamed, "John's been shot. John's been shot." The doorman triggered an alarm and watched in horror as Lennon fell onto the floor of the office, bleeding profusely, his life swiftly slipping away. The doorman called 911 and asked for help to be sent urgently. Yoko and the doorman watched Lennon die.

Outside, Chapman dropped his gun on the sidewalk and calmly walked to the curb. He began reading his copy of *The Catcher in the Rye*. Police arrived and decided they could not wait for an ambulance. Two officers carried Lennon to a squad car as other officers arrived on the scene. Lennon was pronounced dead at 11:07 P.M. but doctors later said that there had been no chance of saving him; his wounds were so severe that he was dead around the time the 911 call was placed. Chapman was taken into custody.

Many Americans would learn of Lennon's death when Howard Cosell broke the news during Monday Night Football. As the New England Patriots prepared for a field goal in a game against Miami, Howard Cosell said, "An unspeakable tragedy, confirmed to us by ABC News in New York City. John Lennon, outside of his apartment building on the west side of New York City, the most famous perhaps of all of the Beatles, shot twice in the back, rushed to Roosevelt Hospital, dead on arrival. Hard to go back to the game after that news flash." He made a similar announcement a little later in the game.

Cosell was right: Lennon was well known and his fame in America was unquestionable. Not only was his work with the

Beatles popular, his recent recordings had been doing well. He was only forty years old and had recently released a much-anticipated album of new music. Lennon was also a resident of New York City and was often seen in and around town, while the other Beatles all still lived in England. Trying to summarize or explain Lennon's importance to music would be impossible and unnecessary here. The real mystery was: Who was Mark David Chapman and why did he kill Lennon?

Chapman's father was in the military and, as a result, Chapman moved around a lot growing up. Born in Texas, he went to high school in Georgia. He achieved poor grades and later claimed he was the victim of bullying. He tried college but dropped out and then ended up working as a security guard. Depressed, he moved to Hawaii. In June 1979, he married, but the marriage did not resolve his problems. He attempted suicide and also began drinking. He confided in friends that he was "going nuts" and became obsessed with the book *The Catcher in the Rye*. He signed letters *Holden Caulfield*, after the book's protagonist. He also became fixated on John Lennon, who famously lived in New York City and occasionally was spotted on the streets, just like anyone else. In October 1980, Chapman traveled to New York City and upon his return told his wife he was going to kill Lennon. Despite his showing her the gun and some bullets he had, she did not warn anyone. She apparently hoped he was getting treatment for mental illness.

Left: The LaLaurie Mansion in New Orleans where "Lady Nero" was rumored to have tortured and murdered her slaves.
*Amanda Baird/
BlackDoll Photography*

Below: The house in which Lizzie Borden allegedly "whacked" her parents.
Lee-Ann Wilber

Right: Author Conrad Aiken's childhood home, the site of a murder-suicide.
Marie Beschen

Below: Eight gruesome murders that took place in this Villisca, Iowa, house in 1912 remain unsolved.
Johnny Houser/ www.villiscaiowa.com

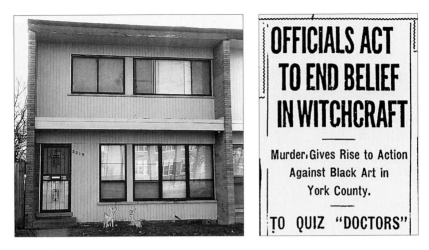

OFFICIALS ACT TO END BELIEF IN WITCHCRAFT

Murder Gives Rise to Action Against Black Art in York County.

TO QUIZ "DOCTORS"

Left: The one-time Chicago apartment where Richard Speck tortured and murdered eight student nurses. *Lupinacci/Campbell*

Right: After a group of angry men murdered Nelson Rehmeyer at his house in 1928, fearing witchcraft, Pennsylvania authorities moved to squelch those beliefs.

Gary Hinman's Topanga Canyon home, where Manson cult members kicked off their murderous spree. *Rachel Reinard*

Serial killer Dean "The Candyman" Corll met his end in the same house in which he murdered as many as twenty-eight boys. *Ken Carter Photography*

Left: The tiny house where James Ruppert shot and killed eleven members of his family. *Lyinn Wolf*

Right: Former peace-activist Ira Einhorn beat his ex-girlfriend to death in the Philadelphia apartment they once shared. *Ed Snyder/StoneAngels.net*

A murder in Savannah's Mercer-Williams House was the subject of the book and film *Midnight in the Garden of Good and Evil.* *C.R.P. Osborne*

Adult film star John Holmes was implicated in the four murders that took place on L.A.'s Wonderland Ave. *Rachel Reinard*

Nicole Brown Smith—O. J. Simpson's ex-wife—and Ronald Goldman were stabbed to death in front of her condominium. *Rachel Reinard*

The murder of child pageant star JonBenet Ramsey in her Boulder, Colorado, home captivated the media. *Rick Pawlenty*

Built in 1704, the General Wayne Inn counted George Washington, Benjamin Franklin, and Edgar Allen Poe among its guests. *Ed Snyder/StoneAngels.net*

The front gates of fashion designer Gianni Versace's Miami Beach mansion. *Courtesy of Steve Lehto*

The Houston, Texas, home where Andrea Yates drowned her five children.
Ken Carter Photography

Was the Gardette-LaPrete
House a sultan's palace?
Not likely. *Jules Loubert*

In December 1980, Chapman again went to New York City. He spent three days hanging around the front of the Dakota. The doorman even became aware of him but considered him harmless. At one point the doorman saw a homeless person ask Chapman for a handout and Chapman gave him ten dollars. Sometimes Chapman wandered away. On December 7, Chapman cornered the musician James Taylor in a subway station and began babbling to him. Taylor found the confrontation off-putting but not terribly out of the ordinary, considering how often he encountered people on the street who recognized him and wanted to talk to him. Chapman appeared to be rambling to Taylor, but later Taylor would tell authorities that Chapman had said he was planning on talking to Lennon as well. Taylor got away from Chapman and chalked it up to just another bad encounter with the public. The next day Chapman would wait outside the Dakota all day, getting Lennon's autograph at one point and then killing him that evening.

News of Lennon's murder shocked America, particularly those who grew up listening to the Beatles. Lennon's album *Double Fantasy* had been released only a couple of weeks earlier. It had neared the top ten of the music charts but sales skyrocketed upon the news. It would hold the number one spot on the album charts for eight weeks in the United States and had similar success overseas. It would win the Grammy for Album of the Year in 1981. People began gathering in front of the Dakota that evening, and a crowd even gathered outside the hospital where Lennon had been taken. Newspeople shot photos and video of onlookers, many of them crying, seemingly confused by the evening's events. The crowd spontaneously began singing the chorus of one of Lennon's songs in unison, "All we are saying is give peace a chance." It was poignant, for Lennon was a well-known pacifist and his violent death seemed to indicate something horribly askew in the universe.

Chapman cooperated with the police and gave them a statement that night, in which he admitted he had shot Lennon but did not give any good reason for doing so. He told them that "part" of him was Holden Caulfield and another part of him was the "devil." Medical authorities examined Chapman to determine if he was competent to stand trial, and they determined he was delusional but not insane. He was charged with murder.

A court-appointed attorney entered a not-guilty plea—by reason of insanity—and prepared to defend Chapman on those grounds. After several psychiatrists and others had examined him, Chapman decided to plead guilty. Chapman's attorney argued to the court that if he was truly insane, his guilty plea should not be accepted by the court. The court listened to arguments from all sides and then determined that Chapman was mentally sound enough to enter the plea and accepted it.

While he had been awaiting trial, Chapman had sent a note to the *New York Times*, telling them to encourage their readers to read *The Catcher in the Rye*. At his sentencing, when asked if he had anything to say, he read a passage from the book to the court. It was the passage where Caulfield describes thousands of children playing in a field of rye near the edge of a cliff and how he would have to stand guard at the edge, to keep children from accidentally falling off the edge. "That's all I do all day. I'd just be the catcher in the rye and all."

The judge sentenced Chapman to twenty years to life, although the maximum sentence was twenty-five to life. It seems unimportant, however. The notoriety of the case guarantees that he will never be paroled. The court also ordered that he be given psychiatric treatment while incarcerated.

The Dakota was originally designed as an apartment building and built in the period between 1880 and 1884. The Dakota Apartments building was supposedly so named after people remarked on the area where it was built. In the 1880s, that portion of New York City was so far away from the city's hub it was considered by many to be in the wilderness. Whether true or not, that is the most commonly told story.

The building is huge. When it was first constructed, it held sixty-five apartments in its ten stories and was aimed at a wealthy clientele. The apartments varied wildly in layout and size, and it was also said that no two were alike. The smallest had only four rooms while the largest had twenty. The building had its own power plant and central heating, both quite unusual for the 1880s. The apartments were all spoken for before construction was completed, and since its opening the Dakota has been known for being a desirable address. The list of famous people who have lived there is robust. Actors and actresses include Lauren Bacall, Jose Ferrer, Judy Garland, Boris Karloff, and Lillian Gish. From television came Connie Chung, Maury Povich, and Gilda Radner. The co-op board famously turned away Melanie Griffith and Antonio Banderas, along with Gene Simmons of the band Kiss, Billy Joel, and Carly Simon. The building has also shown up in many movies such as *Rosemary's Baby* and *Vanilla Sky*. Without a doubt, however, it is most famous as being the home of John Lennon, where he was gunned down in 1980.

As Chapman sits in prison, his name appears in the news from time to time. He has given a few interviews to reporters, and the topic of Lennon's murder seems to surface occasionally as well. For example, in all the confusion after the shooting, the album Chapman had asked Lennon to sign earlier that day got left behind on the sidewalk. Someone found the album and noticed that it bore Lennon's autograph. It was turned over to the police and taken into evidence but was returned to the finder after Chapman was sentenced. The BBC reported that the album was placed for sale by a memorabilia house with an asking price of $525,000. At the time, it was unclear if the album sold, and if it did, what its selling price was or who bought it.

The Dakota is privately owned but visible from the sidewalk and street. It sits on the corner of 72nd Street and Central Park West.

---

* The Editors of *Rolling Stone*, *The Ballad of John and Yoko* (1982).

The House from *Midnight in the Garden of Good and Evil*

THE MERCER–WILLIAMS HOUSE MUSEUM

1981

429 Bull Street
Savannah, Georgia 31401

James Arthur Williams was a prominent antiques dealer who bought and restored many old homes in Savannah, Georgia's historic district. On May 2, 1981, Williams shot and killed his assistant, Danny Lewis Hansford, in the Mercer-Williams House, another grand structure he had resurrected. Williams and Hansford were the only people present in the house at the time of the killing, so the facts remain a bit murky. Prosecutors would argue that Williams and Hansford had been lovers and Williams killed Hansford out of jealousy. Williams said it was self-defense. The story would be rehashed in four murder trials—a record for the state of Georgia—and would end in an acquittal for Williams. And while the legal aspects of the trials would be interesting to some, a bestselling book and then a movie would guarantee this murder house's place in the American consciousness.

Savannah is one of America's most historic Southern cities, having been founded in 1733. Its historic downtown is filled with grand mansions, many built long before the Civil War. It seems fitting that—along with the Conrad Aiken house—it is home to another renowned murder house. Less than a mile from the Aiken House sits the Mercer-Williams House Museum, the site of the Hansford murder. In a city with perhaps a thousand historic buildings, the Mercer was quite well known even before anyone was killed there. And, in the fashion of the Clutter murders and *In Cold Blood*, the crime here was immortalized in a bestselling book and in a Hollywood movie.

The Mercer home is named for the man who began its construction in 1860, a Confederate officer named Hugh Weedon Mercer. Mercer didn't get a chance to live in the house, however. The Civil War broke out before the home was completed. He sold it and let the new owner finish construction, which would not be until 1868. The Mercer name is quite well known in Savannah and elsewhere, but not just because of the house or for the man who had it built. One Mercer who never lived in the house has a story that provides a soundtrack to the events that happened in the house.

John Herndon Mercer, or "Johnny" as he would become professionally known, was the great-grandson of Hugh Mercer. Born in 1909 in Savannah, Johnny became a well-known song-writer, and several of the songs he worked on became American standards. "Hooray for Hollywood" and "Moon River" were just two of the more than 1,500 songs to which he contributed lyrics or music. Many of the songs were for movies, and he was nominated for nineteen Academy Awards and won four. Mercer also co-founded Capitol Records.

As with many neighborhoods in America's larger cities, the one that contained the Mercer house fell out of vogue, and for many years the homes there were not well maintained. In the 1950s, more than a few of Savannah's most historic homes fell victim to the wrecking ball. The Mercer house had been vacant and neglected for a decade when a man named Jim Williams bought it. Williams was well known in Savannah. An antiques dealer, he also refurbished and restored historic homes. He had personally resurrected more than four dozen homes in Savannah's historic districts, homes that had been abandoned and filled blighted and decaying neighborhoods. Some of them would not exist today if Williams had not inter-vened. Williams bought the home for $55,000 in 1969. Before it had been left vacant, it had last been used as a Shriners tem-ple. Williams moved into the Mercer home and spent two years bringing it back to life. When he was done, he remained in it and ran his antiques business from the carriage house on the property. He also hosted extravagant balls at his house for Christmas that were highlights of the Savannah social calendar.

Things were fine until the day in 1981 when Williams shot and killed Danny Hansford. Many people whispered that Hansford was Williams's lover. Williams admitted he had shot Hansford but claimed that Hansford had come at him with a gun and that the shooting was in self-defense. Williams was arrested and posted bond. At first the court asked only for $25,000, but the court soon upped bail to $100,000.

Williams made legal history in Georgia: He was the first person to be tried four times for the same murder. The first trial was in February 1982, where Williams faced a jury of six men and six women. He took the stand and testified in his own defense. It didn't help; the jury returned a guilty verdict after four hours of deliberation. After the conviction, someone sent an anonymous letter to his attorneys pointing out that one of the police officers had contradicted what he had written in his report. The defense attorney had missed it because someone had altered the report before it was given to the defense. Williams appealed and argued that this was grounds for a new trial. The Georgia Supreme Court agreed and granted him a new trial, blaming the errors on the prosecution.

Williams got his new trial in October 1983, and this time the jury was out for only three hours. Still, he was found guilty again and sentenced to a life term in prison. He filed an appeal and complained to anyone who would listen that he was being convicted by the media. Then, a new witnesses came forward with evidence supporting Williams, saying that Hansford had indeed planned to harm Williams. He was granted a third trial. The court released him on $250,000 bond while waiting for trial.

In 1985, John Berendt moved to Savannah to study the story. He had been planning on writing a book about the murder and had been traveling down from New York for visits that lasted a few weeks. The more time he spent in Savannah, the more he realized he needed to live there to observe and absorb the scenery and the characters. He carried a notebook and spent time with the people who would eventually populate his bestseller. Berendt introduced himself to locals saying, "I'm here writing a book." Soon, he became part of the landscape too.

The jury for the third trial, which took place in June 1987, spent four days in deliberation before reporting that they were deadlocked at eleven to one to convict. The prosecution insisted on a fourth trial. At this point, Williams and his attorney appealed to the Georgia Supreme Court, arguing that it was unconstitutional to try him again after a jury had deadlocked on his case. The court didn't buy it. Williams took his case to the U.S. Supreme Court, but they declined to hear it. He would go to trial a fourth time.

This time, the local trial court decided it had had enough. The venue was changed and the trial was conducted a little over 120 miles away, in Augusta, in May 1989. There, a jury found him not guilty, returning their verdict in under two hours. Williams didn't have long to enjoy his freedom; he died less than a year later, in January 1990. He was fifty-nine. His body was found in the Mercer house, in the same room where Hansford had been killed.

The story of the Hansford killing might not have become known outside Georgia if not for the book *Midnight in the Garden of Good and Evil* by John Berendt. In the 1994 work, Berendt took the events of the Hansford killing and wrote a nonfiction novel, much as Capote did with the Clutter murders in his book *In Cold Blood*. Berendt's book hit the bestseller charts and stayed there for an astonishing 216 weeks, going through more than a hundred printings. It sold more than three million copies. The length of time on the bestseller list made it the longest-running bestseller—fiction or nonfiction—of all time.

The book was quickly turned into a movie. Directed by Clint Eastwood, it starred Kevin Spacey as Williams, Jude Law as the man he shot, and John Cusack as the reporter who watched it all unfold, took notes, and then wrote about it later. As with many Hollywood productions, there were hiccups along the way to the silver screen: At one point, producers considered making the character of Berendt a lawyer, to be played by Jodie Foster. Much of the movie was shot in Savannah, including many scenes that were actually shot in the Mercer house. The study where the killing took place was even used in the movie and locals were hired as extras. The movie's premiere was held at the Johnny Mercer Theater in Savannah on November 20, 1997, just six blocks over from the Aiken house, on Oglethorpe Avenue. The soundtrack to the movie featured fourteen songs by Johnny Mercer, including "Skylark," sung by k. d. lang, which was played over the opening credits.

After Williams died, his sister, Dorothy Kingery, moved into the ten-thousand-square-foot home and started operating it as the Mercer-Williams House Museum. Today, visitors can stroll through the home and admire antiques gathered from around the world by Williams. They can see the room where Williams shot a man and then later passed away himself.

The house also contains a gift shop where visitors can buy items commemorating the home's history and its place in the story *Midnight in the Garden of Good and Evil*. The cover of the book features the "Bird Girl" statue, a work by Sylvia Shaw Judson. Judson cast four of the statues and one was placed by a family next to a grave in the Bonaventure Cemetery. *Midnight in the Garden of Good and Evil* featured the Bird Girl on its cover, and soon it was another destination for visitors to the Bonaventure Cemetery. After the Bird Girl had been in the cemetery for more than half a century, the family that had placed her worried that she might not be safe left where she was. They moved her to the Telfair Museum of Art in Savannah. Visitors to the Mercer-Williams House Museum can purchase a miniature replica of the Bird Girl.

Hugh Weedon Mercer, the man who began the construction of the house before he left for the Civil War, is also buried in the Bonaventure Cemetery.

* mercerhouse.com

* "Witnesses: Hansford Never Fired Gun," *Waycross (GA) Journal Herald*, May 9, 1989.

The Dark Side of Hollywood

THE WONDERLAND MURDERS

1981

8763 Wonderland Avenue
Los Angeles, California 90046

On July 1, 1981, around four o'clock in the morning, several people crept into a multilevel home on Wonderland Avenue in the Laurel Canyon neighborhood of Los Angeles. There, they surprised the five occupants of the house and attacked them viciously with pipes. Four of the victims died and the fifth suffered such grievous injuries that she could not recall anything about that horrible night. The gruesomeness of the killings made headlines, but there was even more to the story: The house, which was also believed to be a center of drug dealing, was known as a place where adult movie star John Holmes spent much of his spare time. He claimed he was not there the night of the killings, although he did arrive at his own home shortly after the murders occurred, covered in blood.

There is no other reason to pay special attention to the non-descript house at 8763 Wonderland Avenue in Los Angeles. At the time of the murders, the home was being rented by Joy Audrey Miller but was occupied by a host of unsavory characters, most associated with the drug business. Miller had been arrested seven times. A frequent tenant at the house named Billy DeVerell had been arrested on thirteen occasions. Ronald Launius had done hard time for smuggling drugs; David Lind had been convicted of dealing illegal drugs. The most famous frequent houseguest, however, was John Holmes, a porn star in the twilight of his career. Holmes was thirty-six at the time of the killings and had starred in several thousand adult films.

One of the reasons the Wonderland murders made the headlines was the connection to John Holmes. In Hollywood, where fame and infamy both go a long way, Holmes's work was not exactly respected but he was well known. And when his connection to the Wonderland house was publicized, it caused the case to become a major topic of conversation in Los Angeles.

In his heyday, Holmes had made several thousand dollars a day appearing in hard-core pornographic adult films, but he was well past his prime when the Wonderland murders happened. In later years he had developed an expensive drug habit, freebasing cocaine among other things. As his career had waned, his habit grew and the once physically fit Holmes became scrawny and haggard. Soon, adult film producers were casting him less often, putting him into a financial spiral.

The Wonderland house was an epicenter of drug activity in Los Angeles. The occupants of the house bought, used, and sold drugs, and all were well known to local authorities. Built in 1961, the three-story white stucco house contained a caged metal stairway to the second-floor front door at the time of the murders. The ground floor was the garage. Visitors had to buzz an intercom to get access to the stairs to the upper-floor door. When Holmes and company stayed in the house, the staircase was often guarded by pit bulls. Although Holmes had a wife and a home elsewhere, he spent much of his time at the Wonderland location. To finance his drug habit he often resorted to petty crime, such as stealing luggage from Los Angeles International airport. One of the people he met during his petty-crime career was a drug dealer named Eddie Nash who sometimes helped Holmes unload stolen property.

Drug addicts are not known for making wise decisions. Sometime in 1981, Holmes and some of his friends from the Wonderland address decided to rob Nash. Holmes was scared of Nash, so he devised a plan in which he would get other people to take most of the risk. He would go to Nash's house and buy drugs. When he was there, he would unlock a door at the back of the house and then his friends would come by later and commit the robbery. Holmes figured he would be safe if anything went wrong, since he wouldn't be there when the robbery went down. He was wrong. He bought the drugs from Nash on June 28, 1981. He confirmed to his cohorts that they could get into the home through the unlocked door he had left behind. The next day, four of Holmes's acquaintances from Wonderland stormed into Nash's home and robbed him at gunpoint. They managed to steal quite a bit of cash, jewelry, and drugs. After they left, Nash quickly deduced that the robbers had been helped by a mutual acquaintance, most likely Holmes.

Nash sent some of his henchmen out to find Holmes, and they located him very quickly. He was walking in Hollywood wearing jewelry stolen from Nash. The men dragged Holmes to Nash's house, where he was beaten until he confessed to his role in the robbery, and he soon ratted out the others. The police would later theorize that once Holmes turned on his friends, he had struck a deal with Nash. He would help Nash get revenge on the four men who robbed him and, in exchange, Nash would let Holmes live.

Holmes knew he was lucky to be spared and was willing to agree to anything. Around four A.M., on July 1, 1981, intruders carrying metal pipes invaded the Wonderland home and beat the occupants. Holmes was most likely in the group of attackers, but it is unclear if he participated beyond helping the others get into the house. Five people were staying in the house at the time of the attack, and four of them died. The survivor's injuries were so severe she could not remember anything about the attack and she could not identify the attackers. The four victims were killed savagely, and there was blood everywhere.

Neighbors reported later that they had heard loud noises and screaming coming from the house but had not bothered to call the police; the home was the site of so many late-night parties that this night had sounded just like many other nights at the house.

When the police investigated, one of the things they found at the crime scene was a bloody palm print, which they later matched to John Holmes. Of course, Holmes was known as a frequent visitor to the house, but there was no good reason for his palm print to be in the house in the blood of one of the victims. If he was there, why had he been spared? While the police were wondering about Holmes and what role he might have played in the bloody slaughter, one of the men who had robbed Nash's house and was not present at Wonderland that night called the police and told them of the connection between Nash, Holmes, and Wonderland.

The police searched Nash's house and found, among other things like drugs and money, items stolen from Wonderland. Nash was arrested. Holmes was also arrested, largely because of the bloody palm print he had left at the scene. At this point, the case was becoming quite convoluted. Nash's home had been robbed by the people from Wonderland, and Wonderland had been robbed by Nash's people. Four people were dead. Several trials followed, but the story of the Wonderland murders would never be fully explained.

Prosecutors started with Holmes and tried him for murder. How hard could it be with his bloody handprint at the crime scene? His attorneys admitted that Holmes had been present at the time of the killings but said he was not one of the killers. They said that Nash had forced him to cooperate and if he hadn't cooperated, Nash would have killed him. They said that he was simply brought along as a form of insurance; by placing him at the scene, he would have needed to keep his mouth shut even if he didn't kill anyone. It seemed a risky argument, but the jury found him not guilty.

Once he was acquitted, the prosecutor tried to get Holmes to tell a grand jury what he knew about the murders. After all, if he was there he should be able to tell the police who else was there. And since he had been tried and acquitted, his testimony couldn't hurt him. It didn't matter; he refused to testify anyway. As a result, Holmes was found in contempt and the judge ordered him to be jailed until he was willing to testify. He sat in jail for 110 days. He later claimed that while he was in jail, policemen kept coming by to get his autograph, some bringing in VHS tapes so he could sign the box covers. He eventually agreed to testify but gave the grand jury vague answers. He later said the sketchy testimony was because he was still scared of Nash. In 1985, Holmes was diagnosed with AIDS; he died in 1988, never telling the police what he knew of the Wonderland killings.

Meanwhile, Nash had spent time in prison for drug dealing. After Holmes died, prosecutors announced that they would put Nash and his bodyguard on trial for the Wonderland murders. In a twist possible only in Los Angeles, one of the key witnesses in the Nash trial was Scott Thorson, a former boyfriend of Liberace. Thorson had gotten drugs from Nash shortly before the murders and claimed to have witnessed Nash threatening Holmes over the break-in at Nash's house. The jury in the Nash trial could not reach a verdict because of a lone holdout. They had voted eleven to one to convict Nash. The prosecutor retried Nash, but he was acquitted in the second go-round.

Prosecutors, both state and federal, continued chasing Nash and in 2001, he finally pleaded guilty to sending the men to Wonderland who had committed the murders. He also admitted he had bribed the juror who had held out in his first murder trial, allowing him to be tried the second time, where he had managed an acquittal. And that acquittal meant that he could not be retried for the murders themselves—double jeopardy would prevent that—so he pleaded guilty to conspiracy charges. For good measure, one of Nash's friends also later claimed they had bribed a judge who had agreed to let Nash out of prison after serving only two years of an eight-year sentence for drug dealing. For his role in the Wonderland events, Nash was sentenced to four and a half years in prison.

Much of the story of the Wonderland murders was included in the films *Wonderland*, starring Val Kilmer and Kate Bosworth, and *Boogie Nights*, with Mark Wahlberg and Heather Graham.

The Wonderland house is three stories tall, white stucco, with two levels of living quarters above a garage. It has two bedrooms and two baths and is a little more than a thousand square feet. The lot is 2,500 square feet according to real estate listings. It was built in 1961.

In 2008, various media outlets reported that the Wonderland home was available for a monthly rental of $3,000. According to an ad on Craigslist, it was charming and quaint. "YOU MUST SEE IT!!" The listing gave the address—8763 Wonderland Ave—but did not mention the home's past as the site of a mass murder. If nothing else, the rent had gone up a bit from the $750 a month Joy Audrey Miller was said to have been paying in 1981.

It appears that 8763 Wonderland was often a rental. In 2012 it had an assessed value for tax purposes of $64,304. Zillow, the real estate website, estimated the value of the home at $567,733 in 2012. The home is privately owned but easily visible from the street.

---

* "New Charges in Nineteen-Year-Old Drug Killings in Hollywood," *New York Times*, May 21, 2000.

The Death of John Belushi

CHATEAU MARMONT

1982

8221 Sunset Boulevard, Bungalow 3
Hollywood, California 90046

In March 1982, comedian John Belushi checked into the Chateau Marmont in Hollywood, Bungalow 3. He was in California to party and celebrate his blossoming acting career. He spent his nights at various bars on Sunset Boulevard, drinking and doing drugs. Then he would return to his bungalow to sleep and be roused by a personal trainer who would try to undo the damage Belushi had inflicted on his body the night before. On March 4, he visited a club above the Roxy Theater on Sunset Strip called On the Rox. There, he spent time with a woman named Cathy Smith. Smith was a Canadian rock band groupie who had been linked to members of The Band, Hoyt Axton, and Gordon Lightfoot. Rumor had it that Lightfoot's

"Sundown" was written about her. She met Belushi when The Band had played on *Saturday Night Live*. One reason many rock stars liked her was that she had access to a good supply of drugs. Her nickname was Cathy Silverbag, so named because of the purse in which she was said to carry her stash.

After partying at On the Rox, Belushi was too wasted to drive, so Smith drove him back to his bungalow at Chateau Marmont. She helped him stagger inside. Although he was vomiting, he continued drinking and taking drugs. Around three o'clock in the morning, Robert De Niro and Robin Williams dropped by for a few minutes to visit. After they left, Belushi eventually showered. At 8:00 A.M. he climbed into his bed and went to sleep.

Sometime in those early morning hours of March 5, Smith shot Belushi up with a speedball, which is a mixture of cocaine and heroin. Belushi and Smith were the only people in the bungalow, so no one knows whether Belushi was awake or asleep when Smith gave him the drugs. Although Belushi had a reputation for abusing drugs, he was not known to be a regular user of heroin. Smith became hungry, so she left Belushi to go get breakfast. Rather than order food from the Chateau and have it delivered to the room, she took Belushi's car and went for a drive. Several hours passed. A little after noon, Belushi's personal trainer, Bill Wallace, dropped by looking for Belushi. Wallace, who was also known as "Superfoot" because of his martial arts skills, was a trainer to the stars. A kickboxing champion, he had also trained Elvis Presley. It was his job to try to get Belushi to exercise. He found Belushi lifeless in the bungalow and, after desperately trying to resuscitate him, called for help. Emergency personnel arrived quickly but were far too late. Belushi was pronounced dead at 12:45 P.M. Hollywood law enforcement surveyed the familiar scene and saw cocaine and drug paraphernalia. Meanwhile, Cathy Smith returned from breakfast and walked into the bungalow, now swarming with police and first responders. She played innocent. After all, she hadn't been there when he died.

National news reports soon told of the death of John Belushi, who was only thirty-three years old. Most people immediately guessed how the story had ended: a drug overdose. Belushi's hard-partying ways were well known, although few had expected him to die so young. It was a tragic loss, especially considering the promise his career held at the time.

John Belushi had been one of the most beloved comedians and actors in America in the late 1970s and early 1980s. A regular cast member on *Saturday Night Live* since its beginning, he had starred in the wildly popular *National Lampoon's Animal House*. In 1978, he and Dan Aykroyd had appeared as the musical guests on *SNL* as the Blues Brothers. The act went over so well, the two recorded an album and even toured, selling out huge concert venues. The venture spawned a number one album and a hit movie of the same name based on the fictional characters they were playing. In 1979, Belushi left *SNL* to focus on his film and music careers. He quickly made a few more movies and although they weren't all as successful as

Animal House or *The Blues Brothers*, it was clear that he was a bankable star. Belushi's career wasn't just rising, it was rocketing.

When Belushi checked into Bungalow 3 at the Chateau Marmont, the Chateau was one of the most popular places in Hollywood for the rich and famous to stay. Built in 1927 to resemble a retreat for French royalty called the Chateau d'Ambroise in France, it was initially an apartment complex. The original owner had a hard time keeping tenants in the early years, so he sold the property for $750,000 to a man named Albert Smith, who turned it into a hotel named after the intersection where it sits, at the corner of Sunset Boulevard and Marmont.

Nine cottages were built on the property immediately surrounding the Chateau. In the 1940s, Smith bought them and added them to the hotel. Guests checking into the Chateau have the choice of staying in one of the antique-filled rooms in the seven-story main building or renting one of the bungalows. In all, there are sixty-three rooms, cottages, or bungalows to choose from. Hollywood stars, writers, artists, rock stars, and people who hoped to be famous often stayed at the Chateau, some for extended periods of time. *Architectural Digest* called the property "a real-life version of Rick's café in Casablanca. Everyone who was anyone in Hollywood—or aspired to be— has stayed there, often for weeks or months at a time."

When Smith returned from breakfast the day Belushi died, she was questioned by police and played it fairly cool. She told them she had been with Belushi earlier but made it sound like she had not seen anything important or out of the ordinary. The coroner ruled Belushi's death an accidental drug overdose and Smith went back to Canada. A couple months later, Smith spoke to two reporters from the *National Enquirer*. Not realizing the firestorm the story would cause, she told them everything. The story resulting from that interview was headlined *I Killed Belushi*. Smith admitted to the reporters that she was the one who injected Belushi with the fatal speedball. The story caused an uproar, and authorities in California reversed their position on the death of Belushi. They deemed it a homicide.

Smith was charged with first-degree murder and extradited from Canada. After coming back to Los Angeles, she worked out a plea deal with prosecutors. She pleaded guilty to involuntary manslaughter and served fifteen months in prison. After she was released, Smith was deported to Canada, where she often spoke to schoolchildren about the evils of drugs. Despite her expressions of remorse, she was arrested and convicted of heroin possession in Vancouver in 1991.

John Belushi's death by speedball is just one of many in the celebrity world. The artist Jean-Michel Basquiat, comedians Chris Farley and Mitch Hedberg, and actor River Phoenix all died with some form of heroin and cocaine in their systems. Others barely survived the experience. Dave Gahan, lead singer of Depeche Mode, suffered a heart attack taking the mixture, and Steven Adler of Guns N' Roses suffered a stroke from it.

In 1990, André Balazs bought the Chateau Marmont property and gave it a much-needed restoration. Today, guests can rent the bungalow where Belushi died for around $2,000 nightly, ten times the amount the comedian paid. The Chateau offers amenities that justify the price tag. Private massage therapists and trainers are available, as are secretarial and translation services. Concierge and room service are available twenty-four hours a day.

In August 2012, another famous guest made headlines at the Chateau. Someone leaked a letter to the press that had purportedly been sent by Chateau Marmont management to Lindsay Lohan, the troubled actress whose career had been heading in the wrong direction for a few years. She was in town to shoot a movie for the Lifetime network called *Liz & Dick*. The letter claimed Lohan had checked into the hotel May 30, 2012, and by July 31, her unpaid hotel bill was a little over $46,000. Citing difficulty in getting her to even acknowledge the bill, the hotel told her she had to remove her belongings from her suite and was no longer welcome on their premises. To make matters worse, tabloids got hold of the itemized bill which came with the letter, totaling sixteen pages, detailing what Lohan had done at the hotel to create such a large bill in such a short time. She had accrued charges of over $3,000 in minibar items, $500 in cigarettes, almost $2,000 in restaurant bills, and even $100 for a "Chateau candle," whatever that might be.

Shortly after, Lohan's reps claimed that the brouhaha was caused by a misunderstanding. She had believed that the producers of *Liz & Dick* were going to pick up her expensive tab while she stayed at the Chateau during filming. She apparently settled the bill because it was reported in the news that Lohan was back at the Chateau Marmont, with the blessings of the owner, in the fall of 2012. Her legal problems were far from over, but at least she wasn't banned from Hollywood's hippest hotel, the place where John Belushi was killed.

---

* Ron Harris and Michael Seiler, "John Belushi Dead in Hollywood," *Ottawa Citizen*, March 6, 1982, reprinted from the *Los Angeles Times*.

* Chateau Marmont, chateaumarmont.com

* "Chateau Marmont Revisited," *Architectural Digest*, December 1996.

The Poor Little Rich Kids

THE MENENDEZ FAMILY HOME

1989

722 North Elm Drive
Beverly Hills, California 90210

On August 20, 1989, Kitty and Jose Menendez watched *The Spy Who Loved Me* in the family room of their huge home in Beverly Hills. Kitty was forty-seven years old, Jose forty-four; he was an executive at a movie studio. Before Jose and Kitty Menendez had moved into the property, it had been rented by a variety of other people in the entertainment industry, including Elton John and Prince, for a rumored $35,000 per month. The two fell asleep on the couch in front of the television. Around ten o'clock that evening, someone walked into the living room of the mansion with a shotgun and began shooting the couple. Jose was shot several times, as was Kitty. The killer—or killers—then placed the shotgun barrel up against the back of Jose's head as he lay on the floor and pulled the trigger. In all, the two were shot fourteen or fifteen times. It was gruesome; it was what investigators would call "overkill." The murderers then went around the crime scene and carefully picked up the shotgun shells in an attempt to remove evidence from the scene. Neighbors who heard the shooting said the sound was muffled and did not seem like gunfire. It may be that the sound didn't carry well, or it could have been that the neighborhood was normally so peaceful that no one expected shootings to happen there. The killers vanished without anyone seeing them.

Kitty and Jose did not live alone in the house, although they were the only ones home that evening. They had two adult sons who still lived with them: Lyle and Erik. A few minutes before midnight, the victims' adult children called 911 from the house and, clearly hysterical, barely managed to convey to the operator that someone had killed their parents. During the phone call, one son could be heard yelling at the other. A few minutes later, the police showed up at the house. As they approached the front door, the Menendez brothers came barreling out the door, running right past the police toward the street. There, in the grass by the curb, the two knelt down and sobbed. The police tried questioning them but they were incoherent and uncooperative. The police entered the house and found the bodies of Kitty and Jose, both dead from multiple gunshot wounds.

In 1989, the Menendez murders would seem cut straight from a made-for-TV movie script. The crime would be the center of so much drama it would seem impossible to have actually happened the way it was portrayed in the media. The victims were gruesomely killed by shotgun blasts in their mansion in Beverly Hills. Lyle and Erik would eventually be tried for the murders and sentenced to spend the rest of their lives behind bars as a result. In between the murders and the convictions, there would be twists, turns, and wall-to-wall news coverage of anything to do with the Menendez brothers.

Jose Menendez was an accountant by trade and worked his way up into management of a variety of different companies. The family lived in New Jersey until Jose was offered a job in the entertainment industry in California. His career thrived there too. The family settled in Beverly Hills and the boys, Joseph Lyle and Erik Galen, attended the best schools, traveled extensively, and lived lives of luxury. Erik had dreams of becoming a professional tennis player and often traveled to play in tournaments. Lyle attended Princeton but suffered from bad grades and disciplinary problems, and he wandered back to California. Neighbors noted a series of break-ins around the time the Menendez brothers were both in town.

When the police began investigating on the night of the murders, they quickly noticed that the home had not been robbed and there was no sign of forced entry. Still, they did not suspect the sons at first. They brought the two in for questioning as part of the investigation but could not get much information from them. Erik continued to remain distraught and broke down repeatedly whenever he was questioned about details of the murders. Lyle answered questions but claimed to know nothing about who might have wanted to kill his parents. Some of his answers were odd, though. He told investigators that the house was filled with smoke when they had entered it—even though the investigators never saw any smoke or sign of a fire.

Was he referring to smoke from all the gunfire? If so, it meant they were present in the immediate moments after the gunfire ended. That would contradict the claim the brothers had made that they had come home two hours after neighbors had reported hearing the gunshots, which they had mistaken for the sound of firecrackers. And if they *had* arrived immediately after the shots were fired, why didn't they see the gunmen or hear the shots? After more questioning, the brothers suggested to the police that the killing might have been a mob hit. The police let the brothers go and continued their investigation. The brothers claimed to be so confounded by the crime that they hired a retired police detective to investigate the murders as well.

Perhaps believing they had gotten away with murder, the brothers then began spending their dead parents' money. Jose had a $650,000 personal life insurance policy that named his two sons as beneficiaries. Just four days after the murders, the two spent $15,000 on Rolex watches and jewelry. They bought other expensive things: a $64,000 Porsche and two restaurants. Erik hired a tennis coach and promised him a $60,000 annual salary. They each rented expensive new apartments in the Marina City Towers in Marina del Rey.

The two did not seem to be mourning. At the very least, they were handling the deaths of their parents quite well. They began traveling extensively, to Europe and the Caribbean, and when they were in town, they often drove their mother's Mercedes. They managed to burn through a million dollars in the first six months after the murders and may have been disappointed to find out that their parents hadn't been as rich as they had hoped. While Jose had owned a large portfolio of stock, the real estate owned by Kitty and Jose had been pledged as collateral for large bank loans. Experts suggested that the estate—which the Menendez brothers had hoped was worth tens of millions—might net the boys only $2 million each. But that was assuming they had nothing to do with the murders.

The brothers were also surprised to learn that they wouldn't be receiving an insurance payout through their father's employer. Jose had been the subject of two life insurance policies taken out by the company. One was a "key man" policy that paid his employer a large amount of money if Jose died. The other was a $5 million policy for which Jose could name the beneficiary. When the company took out the two policies, Jose had to submit to a separate physical exam for each. He passed the first physical but hadn't gotten around to taking the second examination before he was killed. As a result, the boys would receive nothing from Jose's personal life insurance policy while the employer would receive $15 million for the key man policy.

After watching the behavior of the sons, the investigators began looking a little more closely at them as possible suspects. They discovered that the boys had hired a computer expert to help them delete something from Kitty's computer shortly after the murders. A friend said that one of the deleted files was a draft of a new will, which had not been as generous to the boys.

Even though Lyle was spending money like a drunken sailor, he was having emotional trouble dealing with the recent events. He decided to talk to a psychologist about his problems. In one of the sessions he confessed to the murders. The psychologist suggested that Lyle should bring Erik in to participate in one of the counseling sessions. When he got there, Erik also admitted his role in the murders but then told the psychologist they would kill him if he told anyone what he had just learned. The psychologist continued meeting with the two on a few more occasions but made sure he kept notes and secretly recorded the sessions. During these meetings,

the brothers discussed the murders at length with the psychologist.

One day, during one of the sessions with the Menendez
brothers, the doctor's girlfriend sat in an adjoining room. She
was waiting for the session to end so she could talk to the psychologist, and she couldn't help but overhear what was happening in the office. The Menendez brothers were yelling at
the psychologist. At one point, she heard one of the brothers
threaten to kill the doctor. Although no violence came of it,
she was worried and she called the police. Now law enforcement had evidence to support their growing suspicions.

The police soon obtained tapes from the psychologist's sessions, and it became clear to them that the Menendez brothers
had killed their parents. Detectives soon hit the pavement,
canvassing stores that sold shotguns, showing cashiers and
salespeople photos of the Menendez brothers. Had anyone
sold a shotgun to them recently? In San Diego County they
found a store that had sold the brothers a pair of shotguns that
fit the crime. The saleswoman would testify that Erik presented a fake ID to purchase a pair of Mossberg 12-gauge shotguns just two days before Kitty and Jose were murdered. The
police decided to arrest the brothers. On March 8, 1990, Lyle
was arrested at the mansion. Erik was out of the country but
turned himself in three days later.

The two still had a good amount of money left, so they
hired the best attorneys money could buy. Erik hired Leslie

Abramson, who specialized in defending death penalty cases, and reportedly paid her $750,000 for her services. Lyle's attorney was reportedly also paid close to three quarters of a million dollars. He was famous too; he had recently defended the "Hillside Strangler." The two would be tried together, but each would have his own jury. The court would have to decide which jury could hear evidence before any given witness testified. Sometimes both juries could hear the testimony; sometimes one jury would hear it while the other jury would get up and leave the courtroom. Simply shuffling the two juries would waste a huge amount of time.

The case soon became a legal quagmire, even before the jury was impaneled. The prosecution wanted to use the tapes and notes from the sessions with the psychologist; defense counsel argued that the materials were doctor-patient privileged. The court made its ruling, which was appealed. The argument ended up in front of the California Supreme Court, which ruled that some of the sessions would be admissible in court—but not all. The Supreme Court ruled that the prosecution could play for the jury portions of the tapes where the brothers threatened the doctor to keep quiet. They would not be able to play the parts where the brothers had detailed how they had committed the murders. Like the Lizzie Borden case—where anyone who read the newspapers knew about evidence that was kept from the jury—most of America believed the Menendez brothers were guilty long before the trial had even started.

One other oddity came to light before the trial. In an article for *Vanity Fair*, Dominick Dunne described a screenplay Erik had written with a friend that he had hoped to sell in Hollywood. Called *Friends*, it was the story of a man who kills his wealthy parents for their inheritance. After writing it, Erik's mother typed the manuscript for him. To many, it looked like Erik had scripted the murder of his parents.

The trial was held in the courtroom of the Honorable Stanley Weissberg, who had recently conducted the trial of the police officers accused of beating Rodney King. It was the verdict from that trial that had preceded the Los Angeles riots after the defendants—four LAPD officers who had been videotaped beating King on the roadside—had been acquitted. Before the Menendez trial began, attorneys for the brothers announced that they were not going to argue that the killings were done by someone else. They were going to admit that they had killed Kitty and Jose because of a lifetime of horrid sexual abuse at the hands of their parents. The outrageous defense guaranteed the trial would generate a huge amount of interest. It was further fueled by a television camera the judge allowed in the courtroom. Almost the entire proceeding was shown live on Court TV.

The trial became a modern-day, real-time soap opera. The prosecution called it a cold-blooded and calculated murder by two spoiled kids who were worried they'd been cut out of their parents' wills. The defense painted Kitty and Jose as violent sexual abusers of their own children. To try to gain sympathy from the jury, the defense attorneys went to great lengths to make Lyle and Erik appear childlike in the courtroom. The brothers were advised to wear sweaters during the trial rather than the suits and ties they had worn at earlier hearings. The defense continually referred to the two men as "boys," and at one point, the judge called Abramson to the bench and admonished her for how touchy-feely she was behaving toward her client in front of the jury. He warned the attorneys to stop acting like "nursemaids or surrogate mothers." Of course, at the time of the murders, both brothers had been adults; Erik had been twenty-one, Lyle eighteen. As the trial dragged on, the brothers took the stand. Their testimony took weeks as they described incredibly deviant sex acts they claimed were perpetrated upon them by their parents.

As expected, the statements the brothers had made to the therapist became central to the prosecution's case. The jury heard Lyle talk about their decision to kill Jose: it "was just a question of Erik and I getting together, and somebody bringing it up, and us just realizing the value in it." Erik was heard saying they had killed their mother because she could never "live without my father." Strangely absent from the tapes were any complaints of sexual abuse.

After closing arguments, the two juries went to deliberate. Erik's jury returned after sixteen days of deliberating and said it was hopelessly deadlocked. Lyle's jury made the same announcement after twenty-four days. The judge thanked the jury members for their service and released them. The district attorney announced that the brothers would be retried. This time the judge said that the two separate juries would not be needed; one jury would decide the fate of both defendants. By now, the Menendez estate was broke and the brothers were declared indigent by the court. Abramson was paid by the state of California to continue representing Erik, but she would not be getting such a hefty paycheck this time around. Lyle was appointed counsel through the public defender's office. And this time, perhaps wondering it if might help speed the trail along, Judge Weissberg decided there would be no television cameras in the courtroom. This trial lasted almost half a year. Erik testified for fifteen days. The defense was essentially the same. The brothers claimed they blasted their parents to death with shotguns because they felt that somewhere down the road, Kitty and Jose were going to kill them.

The jury must have been exhausted by the time the trial came to an end. The prosecutor's closing argument lasted three and a half days. The defense attorneys weren't quick either. This time, the jury found the brothers guilty on all charges and also found that special circumstances existed, which meant the brothers would get life in prison with no parole or the death penalty. After a lengthy penalty-phase hearing, the jury opted to not have the brothers executed. It was 1996, almost seven years after they had killed their parents, when they finally went to prison.

The Menendez brothers fought the convictions. After

exhausting their appeals in the California state court system, they turned to the federal courts. There, they argued that they were denied a fair trial because the trial court hadn't let them put in more evidence of how scared they were of their parents. In other words, if the Menendez brothers got another trial, it would be longer than the previous two. They also thought it was unfair that the jury got to hear the tapes made by the therapist. The federal courts didn't agree with their take on the law. In 2005, the Ninth Circuit Court of Appeals denied their request to be freed.

What little was left of the estate of Kitty and Jose Menendez was finally liquidated and the home where Kitty and Jose had been killed was sold before the sons were finally convicted.

The house where the Menendez brothers killed their parents is located at 722 North Elm Drive in Beverly Hills, California. It is Mediterranean in style, the roof is red tile, and it was built in 1927. In 1974, it had been remodeled and updated. It sits on a half-acre lot and is a little over nine thousand square feet, with six bedrooms and eight baths. It sold in 2001 for $3,743,000 and is privately owned today.

A swimming pool and a guesthouse are behind the house. It is possible that the guesthouse played a role in the murders. In his *Vanity Fair* article, Dunne noted that he believed it was likely that the killers had gone to the guesthouse and showered before leaving the premises. The guesthouse is two stories tall and even has its own two-car garage. Behind the property was an alley. A person could drive a car from the alley into the guesthouse garage without neighbors on Elm seeing the car coming or going.

---

* "Jury Recommends Life without Parole," *The (Youngstown, OH) Vindicator*, April 18, 1996.

* Dominick Dunne, "The Menendez Murder Trial," *Vanity Fair*, October 1993.

The Suburban Serial Killer

JOEL RIFKIN

1993

1492 Garden Street
East Meadow, New York 11554

In March 1989, thirty-year-old Joel David Rifkin was left home alone when his mother went on a trip out of town. He celebrated his freedom by hiring a prostitute in the East Village and bringing her to the house he shared with his mother in East Meadow, about a half hour east of Manhattan. After they engaged in sex, he bludgeoned and strangled her to death. He dragged her body into the basement, where he dismembered her with an X-Acto knife, chopped off her head, and placed it in a paint can. He cut off her fingertips and pulled out her teeth, hoping to make her remains impossible to identify. He then drove around, scattering her body parts in a variety of places. Despite his careful efforts, someone stumbled upon the head in the can within a few days and the story hit the papers. As he had hoped, the police could not identify her, but Rifkin was spooked. He didn't kill again for a year. But then he couldn't help himself. It would be four gruesome years before the police caught him, and by that time he would have killed quite a few more times.

A little after 3:00 A.M. on June 28, 1993, Rifkin was driving his Mazda pickup truck on Long Island when a police officer noticed the truck was missing a license plate. The officer activated his flashing lights but Rifkin kept driving. When the officer used his public address and told Rifkin to pull over, Rifkin veered toward the next exit and floored the accelerator. He led the police—the initial officers were soon joined by others on the empty streets—on a wild chase that lasted twenty minutes. It came to an end when Rifkin lost control of his truck and ran into a telephone pole.

As the police approached, Rifkin calmly got out of his truck. The police asked him for identification and noticed that he had Noxzema slathered across his mustache. As they tried to make sense of the sober thirty-four-year-old man who had led them on a high-speed chase, one of the officers noticed a foul smell coming from the bed of the truck. Under a blue tarp was the nude body of a woman who had been dead for several days. Rifkin had apparently smeared the Noxzema under his nose so that he could handle the corpse without being overcome by the stench of rotting flesh. When the police asked him to explain the presence of the dead woman in the back of his truck, Rifkin said, "She was a prostitute. I picked her up on Allen Street in Manhattan. I had sex with her, then things went bad and I strangled her. Do you think I need a lawyer?"

The police arrested Rifkin. At the police station, they learned that Rifkin lived at 1492 Garden Street in East Meadow, with his sister and his seventy-one-year-old mother. The police called Mrs. Rifkin to tell her that her son was in police custody after a car accident. They were not sure how much she might know about what her son had been doing while she was out of town, so they were being cautious. They didn't want to tip her off if she knew anything, and they didn't want to alarm her if she didn't. As he was being interrogated, Rifkin told the police that the woman in the back of his truck— her name was Tiffany Bresciani—was his seventeenth victim. The police quickly obtained a search warrant for the Rifkin home, and soon they had no doubt Rifkin was telling the truth. Understanding how Rifkin had gotten to the point where he could so callously kill and chop up prostitutes would take a little longer.

Both Rifkin and his sister had been adopted. Rifkin had been a high school outcast, and later as an adult, a loner. The only jobs he ever managed to keep involved tasks he could do outdoors and largely by himself, such as landscaping. He could not master jobs that involved human interaction. After high school, Rifkin had tried attending college—several colleges, actually—but had dropped out of each one after performing miserably in classes. Although he made halfhearted attempts to move out of his mother's house, he never quite launched. He worked sporadically but was often fired for incompetence. What little money he earned, he spent on prostitutes.

The Rifkin home was owned by Joel's mother, and police showed her the search warrant. In her son's bedroom, police found photos of women that Rifkin had kidnapped, women's jewelry, and numerous items associated with women, such as makeup cases, wallets, purses, and driver's licenses. Police suspected they were souvenirs Rifkin had taken from his victims. Two pieces of identification belonged to women whose bodies had been found in 1991 and 1992. He also had books about mass murderers in his bedroom. Items found in Rifkin's room would help the police solve a dozen or more open murder cases in the area. As the search continued, it became clear that Mrs. Rifkin was unaware of the things her son was doing in the house when she wasn't home, and she had never gone into his room to see his bizarre collection of souvenirs from the women he had murdered.

The garage of the home contained more gruesome evidence. Much of it was mixed in with Rifkin's landscaping tools. A wheelbarrow had blood and human flesh in it. There was a pair of women's panties on the floor, not far from more tarps and ropes. Realizing that the police had found more than enough evidence to pin dozens of murders on him, Rifkin began giving details of the many women he had killed. He described how he would drive into Manhattan and find prostitutes willing to travel back to East Meadow, often when his mother was not at home. There, in the house, he would have sex with them and then kill them, often beating them to death. He dismembered some of them; others he simply hauled out of the house and dumped. He would throw them in rivers, canals, or wooded areas in New Jersey and New York. Some of the victims would never be found. Others were found almost immediately as Rifkin scattered his victims around the area. And a few of the women were killed in his truck.

Rifkin's life story was remarkable in that he seemed to be a target of bullying at every turn. He was even robbed by hookers quite a few times, and one working girl managed to run off with his money—before earning it—twice. Rifkin could only stand for so much bullying, however. He had not lashed out at the kids who tormented him in school. He struck back at the prostitutes.

Rifkin had killed his first prostitute when his mother left town in 1989. He waited a year before killing again. Then, Rifkin's mother left town and Joel brought another prostitute home. After killing her, he chopped up her body but decided he could not risk having the body parts found like last time. He bought cement and used it to weight down the body parts of his victim, which he then threw into the East River. That victim was never found, although later Rifkin would confess enough of the details for her to be identified. Rifkin admitted to killing her because the police had found her diary in Rifkin's bedroom, and she had been reported missing.

From that point forward, he began killing more often. He would pick up prostitutes and take them home at first. Later, as he escalated the intensity of his crimes, he would cut to the chase and just kill them in his vehicle. He wouldn't always bother taking steps to hide the bodies very well, either. He dumped victims in and around New York City, or sometimes he would leave them in New Jersey. Many of his victims would not be reported missing for months, if at all.

His last victim's odyssey was bizarre, as the police would later find out when they heard Rifkin explain how he had come to have Bresciani in the back of his pickup truck the morning he was apprehended. He had met her early in the morning of June 24, 1993, and strangled her while they were parked in the parking lot of the *New York Post*. He was driving his mother's car while she was out of town, so he put the body in the backseat and headed home. On the way, he stopped and bought a tarp. He wrapped his victim in the tarp and placed her body in the trunk. It was a lucky move on his part. When he got home he found out that his mother had returned from her trip early and she needed her car to go shopping. Mrs. Rifkin went and ran her errands without ever realizing that the dead body of a murder victim was in the trunk of her car. When she returned, Joel pulled the body from the trunk and placed it in the wheelbarrow in the garage. He left it there for three days. It was then that he decided to take the body and dump it on Long Island—where he encountered the police who pulled him over for having no license plate on his truck.

Despite admitting to so many murders, Rifkin forced the state to put him on trial. He had decided it was worth a shot at trying to convince a jury he was insane. Prosecution experts agreed that he had mental problems, but not enough to exonerate him for his killing spree. The defense experts weren't persuasive enough. The jury convicted him of two murders. He then pleaded guilty in the other cases against him. By the time the dust settled, Rifkin was sentenced to 203 years in prison. One of the judges who passed sentence on him said in court, "It is not in my power to give Mr. Rifkin the sentence he deserves. In case there is such a thing as reincarnation, I want you to spend your second life in prison." Rifkin will be eligible for parole in 2197.

As is so often the case with prisoners given impossibly long jail sentences, Rifkin got tired of his stay in prison and began filing appeals. His attorneys argued that Rifkin's convictions should be overturned because he had made some statements to the police before he had been advised of his rights. It was a long shot: The police had found the dead woman's decomposing body in the back of his pickup truck before he had said anything incriminating. And the body had been in plain view of the officers at the scene of the traffic stop. The New York courts didn't agree with Rifkin's argument. One judge indicated that there might have been some slight irregularities in his trial, but the rest of the evidence was so overwhelming it would not have made a difference if the prosecution had been forced to try the case without Rifkin's statements being used against him.

The house Rifkin lived in at the time of his arrest was owned by his mother, Jeanne Rifkin. His father had died in 1987. After being diagnosed with prostate cancer the previous year, he took an overdose of barbiturates. He died a few days later in a hospital. Rifkin had killed and dismembered several of his victims in the house. His mother was not involved in any way with the crimes, and she continued living in the house after Rifkin was sentenced to prison. She passed away in March 2010 and the home was placed on the market. The listing called it an "excellent handyman's special."

> This two-story expanded ranch features a nice open
> floor plan, hardwood floors, four nice-size bedrooms
> and two lovely bathrooms. Great home, located in a
> wonderful neighborhood and in the superb Barnum
> Woods School District. All buyers welcome.

The house had been built in 1951. The local news soon picked up on the story and some wondered if a buyer could be found for so notorious a house. Real estate agents pointed out that there was no law in New York state requiring disclosure of a house's murderous past, but would someone really be able to sell this house without the buyer knowing? It was a timely question; at that moment, the DeFeo "Amityville Horror" house was also for sale. Lawyers told the press that while state law did not require disclosure of the house's past, one could not simply lie to a prospective purchaser. In other words, if someone asked, they had to be told. In response to lawsuits in some states brought by aggrieved buyers of murder homes—and others that were "stigmatized" by events at the home—some states passed laws addressing these questions. However, most of the laws protected sellers and brokers who failed to disclose the stigmatizing event. This area of the law became so muddled and confusing—most people assumed the laws required sellers and brokers to disclose—that numerous articles appeared in real estate and law review publications in an attempt to lend guidance.

While the Rifkin name may have slowed the sale of the house, eventually a buyer was found. It finally sold in 2011 for $322,000, a tad under the asking price of $349,000 with which it had first been listed. The local newspapers wrote about the sale of the house and interviewed the new owners, a couple who asked that their last names not be published. The wife told a reporter that she was a teacher, and "It's a great house and we got it for a great price." Asked about the ugly history of the home, she and her husband knew "something happened in the house," but it didn't bother them. Her husband said, "A house is a house. People die all the time in houses. We're bringing all positive vibes."

---

* "Landscaper Admits to a Dozen Killings, Police Say," *New York Times*, June 29, 1993.

Getting Away with Murder

NICOLE BROWN SIMPSON
AND RONALD GOLDMAN

1994

879 South Bundy Drive (formerly 875 South Bundy Drive)
Los Angeles, California 90049

Nicole Brown Simpson lived in a condominium with two children she had with her ex-husband, Hall of Fame football player, O. J. Simpson. The condo was in a neighborhood of Los Angeles referred to as Brentwood; O. J. lived two miles away, at 360 North Rockingham, also in Brentwood. On June 12, 1994, Nicole went out to dinner at a local restaurant called Mezzaluna, and her mother, who was dining with her, left her sunglasses behind when the two left after their meal. A waiter at the restaurant who knew Nicole, Ronald Goldman, offered to bring the sunglasses to her condo.

Goldman and Nicole stood outside the front door of the condo talking, in an area that was secluded because of the foliage on the property. Someone walked around the side of the building from the alley behind the condo and confronted the two. A violent struggle followed. The intruder used a knife to stab both Nicole and Goldman, brutally killing both of them. A few minutes after midnight—early on the morning of June 13—Goldman and Nicole were found by neighbors who had been alerted by the barking of Nicole's dog. The two victims lay in pools of blood in front of the Bundy condominium's front door.

Nicole's condo had a partially hidden walkway that led to its front door and, judging by a single set of bloody footprints that did not belong to either victim, the police concluded that one person had killed both Nicole and Goldman on the walk. A narrow walkway also leads to the alley behind the condo, which was most likely the escape route used by the killer. In two trials—one criminal and one civil—and endless media coverage, the facts of what happened in front of the condo were discussed ad nauseam. While some of the facts may have been debatable, underlying all of it were two gruesome killings. One particular wound to Nicole's neck almost decapitated her, cutting clean through to her vertebrae. She was also stabbed in the head and neck several times. Goldman was stabbed as many as thirty times and left to die on the sidewalk. Then, according to a witness, the killer sped off in a white Bronco, toward Rockingham. Inside the condo, Nicole's two young children, aged nine and six, were still sleeping.

O. J. Simpson's murder trial was another one labeled as

the Trial of the Century by the news media. Judging by the amount of press coverage it received, it certainly was a legitimate contender for the title. Orenthal James Simpson was a well-known athlete and celebrity, having launched his career by playing football at the University of Southern California. There, he led the NCAA in rushing yardage for two years and won the Heisman Trophy, along with a variety of other accolades. He went to the National Football League, where he stacked up rushing and scoring records at Buffalo and San Francisco. He retired in 1980 and was elected to the NFL Hall of Fame the first year he was eligible.

Simpson then turned to acting and found roles in *Roots*, *The Towering Inferno*, and the *Naked Gun* films, among others. He also worked as a sports broadcaster. At times, he seemed ubiquitous, landing lucrative endorsement deals that placed him in commercials as well. He pitched everything from Hertz car rentals to—of course—orange juice. He appeared good-natured and friendly. Everyone seemed to like him.

In 1977, Simpson met a woman almost twelve years his junior named Nicole Brown. Nicole was a waitress at a Beverly Hills nightclub. Simpson was married but would divorce his wife in 1980. Simpson had been working in Hollywood more as he began planning his exit from football and had even appeared in a few big-screen projects, although not all of them were blockbusters. Around this time he made a movie called *Detour to Terror* where he played the lead. Nicole had an uncredited role in the film as a bus passenger. In 1985, Simpson married Nicole Brown. The couple had two children but separated and then divorced in 1992. It would later become well known that Nicole had filed domestic violence charges against Simpson during their separation, charges to which Simpson had pleaded no contest.

Los Angeles police investigating the two murders at the Bundy condominium quickly turned their attention to Simpson as a suspect. He was known to have had a troubled and violent relationship with his ex-wife, and the evidence soon began piling up against him. When they called to tell him his ex-wife had been killed, he did not ask the detective any details of the murder. He didn't even bother to ask which of his two ex-wives had been killed. Simpson owned a white Bronco and a witness said she saw a white Bronco speeding away from the crime scene. She identified the driver as O. J. Bloody footprints at the scene matched Simpson's footwear. A bloody glove was found at Simpson's Rockingham residence. Bloody socks were found in Simpson's bedroom. Blood inside Simpson's Bronco and on his clothing matched both Simpson and Nicole.

Simpson's attorneys told the police that they could avoid a media circus by letting Simpson turn himself in rather than having him arrested. The police agreed and told the attorneys that Simpson should present himself to the police by 11:00 A.M. on June 17. Simpson did not show. His attorneys held a press conference and read a letter that Simpson had written, in which he stated that he did not kill Nicole and that he had lived a good life. Many people thought it sounded like a suicide note, something the attorneys did not contest. The police announced they were going to arrest Simpson if they found him alive. The city of Los Angeles was abuzz. Where was O. J.?

Around 6:30 that evening, someone notified the LAPD that Simpson's white Bronco was on the 405 freeway near L.A. Soon, police were following the vehicle and helicopters flew overhead to give television viewers live coverage. Al Cowlings, a former teammate of Simpson's, was driving the Bronco, and when a squad car pulled even with the vehicle, Cowlings told the officers to get away because Simpson was in the backseat with a gun to his own head. The police moved back and contented themselves with following the Bronco in what became the iconic slow-motion Bronco chase.

Eventually, Simpson drove to his Rockingham home in Brentwood, where he sat in his Bronco in the driveway for forty-five minutes before going into his house for an hour. He then surrendered to police. When police searched his Bronco, they found $8,750 cash, the gun he had been holding to his head, his passport, a disguise, and a change of clothing. It was later estimated that almost a hundred million people watched some or all of Simpson's escapades that night, which had been broadcast live on ABC, NBC, CBS, and CNN.

The extensive coverage of the chase was a precursor to what became one of the longest and most publicized trials in American history. Simpson hired a very expensive team of lawyers—someone dubbed them "the Dream Team"—and he pleaded "absolutely, one hundred percent, not guilty" to two murder charges. Jury selection began in October 1994, and the trial itself began January 24, 1995. Almost all of the proceedings were broadcast live on the Court TV cable channel and most nightly newscasts on the major networks carried updates from the trial as part of their regular news. The trial was on television for a total of 133 days. Simpson spent several million dollars hiring his nine attorneys, and they defended him by arguing that the mountain of evidence facing O. J. was fraudulent or somehow flawed due to police ineptitude and misconduct.

One aspect of the case puzzled many people and still is the source of much confusion. The case was tried in the downtown Los Angeles court rather than the court in Santa Monica, which was technically the court closest to the crime scene. Any other crime committed in that neighborhood would have been tried in Santa Monica. And each court drew its potential jurors from within the area around the court. Why did they choose to try the case downtown? Many people assumed that the district attorney had made the conscious decision to try the case with a more racially diverse jury. The district attorney never explained the rationale behind the trial's location, but the California appeals court judge who oversaw that district later told a reporter that the decision had not been made by the prosecutor. It had been made by court administrators and the prosecutor had simply not explained the process publicly. At the time, the downtown court was better equipped to handle the expected media crush. The Santa Monica courthouse had also been recently damaged by an earthquake and was in need of repair. Still, there is no question that a jury from Santa Monica would probably not have been as racially mixed as one from downtown. The recent Rodney King trial had preceded some ugly events, and it had been an all-white jury sitting in judgment on a matter of race.

During the trial there were fireworks, but they were overshadowed by the sheer volume of evidence presented. The prosecution called seventy-two witnesses. There were even a few more they should have called but couldn't. One was the woman named Jill Shively who said she saw Simpson fleeing the scene in his white Bronco. She testified before the grand jury and was to be a key witness until she sold her story to *Hard Copy* and a tabloid for a combined $30,000. Prosecutors had told her to not speak to the press before she testified, but she had found the easy money too tempting. Likewise, Jose Camacho testified before the grand jury that he had sold Simpson a large knife just a few weeks before the murder. Prosecutors believed this was the murder weapon, but Camacho reportedly accepted $12,500 to sell his exclusive story to the *National Enquirer*.

There were also mistakes made by the prosecution. The biggest blunder of all was the prosecution asking Simpson to try on the gloves found the night of the murder. The gloves had been soaked in blood and dried, and Simpson was asked to put rubber gloves on first, then to try pulling the dried-blood-infused gloves over them. The gloves wouldn't fit.

One of the last famous quotes from the trial was delivered by Johnnie Cochran, Simpson's attorney. Referencing the bloody gloves that Simpson couldn't squeeze over another pair of rubber gloves in the courtroom, Cochran told them, "If it doesn't fit, you must acquit." By the time the case got to the jury—October 3, 1995—most Americans had formed opinions of Simpson's guilt. It mattered very little, though. The jury found him not guilty after only three hours of deliberation.

Simpson was later sued on behalf of the two murder victims' estates, and a civil jury ordered Simpson to pay $33.5 million for killing Goldman and Nicole. Despite the best efforts of the attorneys for the victims, very little of the judgment has been paid. Afterward, Simpson moved to Florida where he had further scrapes with the law, but his luck started turning on him. In 2006, it was announced that Simpson had written a book describing how he would have committed the murders hypothetically, titled *If I Did It*. The publisher had also swung a deal for Simpson to appear on a television special with the Fox network to be called, "If I Did It, Here's How it Happened." A storm of outrage and public criticism soon caused the publisher to cancel the book's publication, and the television special was also scrapped. After some legal wrangling, the Goldman family—who still held the largely unpaid judgment against Simpson—acquired the rights to the book and published it with a cover design that downplayed the word *If*, making it appear to read *I Did It*.

Then, in September 2007, Simpson was involved in a bizarre incident at a Las Vegas hotel where he and several accomplices entered the room of another man and grabbed sports memorabilia that they claimed was owned by Simpson. Simpson denied it, but the men with him would later testify that they had used a gun in the incident. Simpson claimed he was simply retaking possession of items that had been stolen from him. It is unclear why, if the victim really was in possession of Simpson's stolen property, Simpson couldn't just call the police.

The jury in his Las Vegas case was not as understanding of Simpson as the jury had been in the Goldman-Brown case in Los Angeles. He was found guilty of all charges, including kidnapping and armed robbery, and in December 2008 he was sentenced to a thirty-three-year prison term. He has the possibility of parole after nine years. After the trial in Los Angeles, the condo where Nicole and Goldman were murdered was placed on the market for a little under $800,000. Over two years, the price was gradually reduced, and eventually someone bought the condo for $590,000, substantially less than what it probably would have been worth without the notoriety. The new owners changed the address and overhauled the property's appearance. In 2006, the condo sold again for almost $1.7 million. The notoriety seemed to be wearing off. O. J.'s mansion on Rockingham, where police had found socks soaked in Nicole's blood and a bloody glove, was sold by Simpson. The new owner razed everything on the property, including the main house.

In 2012, the Discovery Channel aired a documentary called *My Brother the Serial Killer*, about a convicted killer named Glen Rogers. Rogers was convicted of murdering a woman in Tampa but claimed that he had also been the one who killed Nicole Brown and Ronald Goldman. According to the documentary, Simpson asked Rogers to go to the Bundy condo and steal a pair of $20,000 earrings. According to Rogers, Simpson told him to kill Nicole if necessary. While O. J. was reportedly delighted that the documentary had been made and aired, the families of the victims condemned it as being inaccurate and said that Rogers was just seeking attention. At the time the documentary aired, he was on death row in Florida. According to police, he admitted to killing seventy women but authorities do not believe he killed anyone at the Bundy condo. An official from the Los Angeles Police Department was quoted as saying, "The LAPD is quite confident that we know who killed Nicole Brown Simpson and Ron Goldman. We have no reason to believe that Mr. Rogers was involved." They also pointed out that the two murders at Bundy did not match the behavior of Rogers in his other killings.

Then why might someone claim to be the one who killed two people? When he made the claim, Rogers was on death row in Florida and had exhausted all of his appeals. Perhaps he was hoping California might decide to investigate his claims and delay his execution in the meantime.

Meanwhile, the Bundy condominium is privately owned and the front walk is getting increasingly overgrown, perhaps to keep prying eyes away.

---

* Vincent Bugliosi, *Outrage: The Five Reasons Why O. J. Simpson Got Away with Murder* (2008).

* Jeffrey Toobin, *The Run of His Life* (2013).

The Unsolved Christmas Murder
of the Child Beauty Queen

JONBENÉT RAMSEY

1996

755 15th Street (now 749 15th Street)
Boulder, Colorado 80302

One of the most controversial and well-known murder cases in America took place in a huge house in Boulder, Colorado, at Christmastime 1996. JonBenét Ramsey was a six-year-old girl who lived with her parents, John and Patsy Ramsey, and her older brother, Burke. The morning after Christmas, Patsy came downstairs and found a ransom note on the stairs to the kitchen. The note indicated that JonBenét had been kidnapped and was being held for ransom. Patsy found JonBenét's room empty and quickly took action. The Ramseys notified the police and began taking steps to obtain the ransom money.

The police had been called shortly before 6:00 A.M. and

soon arrived and began preparing for what they assumed would be negotiations with the kidnappers. After they had set up and briefed everyone, an officer suggested that John Ramsey and a friend should look through the rest of the house thoroughly to see if there was any evidence that might help them. It had been six hours since the police had arrived. The house had several floors and a convoluted floor plan, so an extensive search of the house would actually take a good amount of time.

After going through a few rooms, the two men entered a room in the basement. There they found the lifeless body of JonBenét. She had been strangled and her skull was fractured. John Ramsey, reacting instinctively, removed tape that had been placed over his daughter's mouth and then carried her body upstairs. It was later determined that she had probably been dead since late the night before. Detectives would only be able to speculate about the crime scene since it had been disturbed when JonBenét's father had carried her upstairs.

JonBenét was the one and only murder victim in Boulder in 1996, and much of what the police did next appeared to be the result of simple incompetence. After the Ramseys had called the police, they also called friends for help. The house was the scene of a lot of activity and foot traffic and was not secured as a crime scene until after the body had been found. The contaminated crime scene did not seem to bother the police all that much, though. They would focus almost exclusively on the Ramseys as their murder suspects. What followed became a media circus fueled by law enforcement leaks and rabid tabloids.

Tabloids revealed that JonBenét had competed in child beauty pageants, and newspapers and television talk shows soon splashed images of the six-year-old JonBenét strutting in front of judges on stages, made up and dressed like an adult beauty queen with coiffed hair, heavy makeup, and fancy evening gowns. The images, of a child made up as an adult, stunned many Americans who had no idea that beauty pageants even existed for little children. Many people made the leap in their minds that JonBenét's mother must have been a domineering stage mother to push a child into pageants at such a young age. Worse, the papers soon began reporting that the Ramseys were the only suspects in the case as far as the police were concerned. Unsure of how to handle the media glare, the Ramseys hired an attorney. Although they continued to cooperate with law enforcement, the Ramseys were criticized for hiring legal assistance, which many people assumed was a sign of belligerence—or guilt—on the part of the family.

Several oddities about the case confounded investigators. The ransom note demanded $118,000, an unusual amount of money that was almost exactly the same as a bonus John Ramsey had recently received at work. How many people would have known that? The note claimed it had been written on behalf of "a group of individuals that represent a small foreign faction." No other clues to the writer's identity were given; the note was signed *Victory! S.B.T.C.* Investigators hinted that the note appeared to have been written by Patsy Ramsey, although handwriting experts with law enforcement quietly admitted they could not make any such conclusion.

Pressure mounted on the Ramseys to speak to the press, which they eventually did, giving an interview to CNN. Patsy famously told the interviewer, "There is a killer on the loose. I don't know who it is, I don't know if it's a he or a she but if I were a resident of Boulder I would tell my friends to keep their babies close to you." The very next day the mayor of Boulder held a press conference in response to Patsy's statement. She said, "People in Boulder have no need to fear that there is someone wandering the streets of Boulder, as has been portrayed by some people, looking for children to attack. Boulder is safe, it's always been a safe community and it continues to be a safe community." Her message was clear: The Ramseys had killed JonBenét. The Colorado governor even said the Ramseys ought to "quit hiding behind their attorneys [and] quit hiding behind their PR firm."

The investigation dragged on. Even though the police focused on the Ramseys, they were hard-pressed to come up with clues or a motive. They had theories but no evidence linking the parents to the killing. The case stymied investigators. A grand jury was called and took testimony, even calling JonBenét's brother to the stand. The grand jury prepared indictments naming the Ramseys of "two counts each of child abuse resulting in death in connection to the first-degree murder of their six-year-old daughter," but the district attorney refused to sign it, saying the evidence was not sufficient to support the charges. The actions of the grand jury were secret, however, and the public was not told about any of this until 2013. Eventually, the Ramseys moved out of the home.

Patsy Ramsey passed away from ovarian cancer in June 2006. In August of that year, the case was thrust back into the headlines when a man came forward and claimed he was somehow involved in JonBenét's death. John Mark Karr was a forty-one-year-old former teacher who was being sought on child pornography charges out of California. Authorities tracked him to Thailand and brought him back to the United States. Somewhere along the way he told authorities he had been present when JonBenét had died but that her death was an accident. The claim rekindled the media frenzy surrounding the case; some headlines screamed that the case was solved and that Karr was the culprit. But authorities found Karr's story unbelievable after they began checking the details. Apparently he could not convince them that he was ever inside the Ramsey's house, and his DNA did not match a sample found at the crime scene. Karr was later released, apparently not even being prosecuted for the original charges that had brought him to the attention of the authorities in the first place. The police had originally charged Karr with possession of child pornography after they said they had found such images on his computer, which they seized. By the time Karr had been taken into custody and made his claims about JonBenét, the police had lost the computer that had been the basis of the charges against him.

Two years later, officials announced that neither of the Ramseys had been involved in the murder of JonBenét. Advances in testing had allowed for the identification of small amounts of DNA recovered from the crime scene. The DNA did not match anyone in the family and belonged to someone as yet unknown to police. The profile has been placed into the FBI database, which is checked every few weeks. It is possible Jon-Benét's killer will be identified one day after a routine search of the database, but until then, the trail remains cold.

Upon receiving the results of the DNA testing, the Boulder district attorney did the unheard-of and issued a written apology to John Ramsey. After outlining the DNA conclusion, the letter stated: "To the extent that we may have contributed in any way to the public perception that you might have been involved in this crime, I am deeply sorry. No innocent person should have to endure such an extensive trial in the court of public opinion, especially when public officials have not had sufficient evidence to initiate a trial in a court of law." The letter went on to state that the district attorney's office would handle such situations differently in the future. Of course, the letter came too late for Patsy Ramsey, who had gone to her grave proclaiming her innocence.

The home where JonBenét Ramsey was murdered was built in 1972 and is 7,240 square feet. It sits on a quarter-acre lot and contains three fireplaces along with five bedrooms and six and a half baths. The Ramseys sold it for $650,000 to an investment group, which then resold the house and donated the profits to the JonBenét Ramsey Children's Foundation. In May 2004, a new family moved in. More recently, the house was listed for sale with an asking price of $1.985 million. The address of the house has been changed to limit gawkers, but they still come by. Perhaps eventually people will stop driving by and having their pictures taken in front of the house where the little beauty queen was murdered.

---

* Mary George, "DA Says He'll Wait for Evidence," *Denver Post*, February 28, 1997.

* Karen Ange and John Ingold, "DA Clears Ramsey Family," *Denver Post*, July 10, 2008.

* Kirk Mitchell and John Ingold, "JonBenét Ramsey Grand Jury Indictment Accused Parents of Child Abuse Resulting in Death," *Denver Post*, October 25, 2013.

Murdered in the Haunted Inn

THE GENERAL WAYNE INN

1996

625 Montgomery Avenue
Merion, Pennsylvania 19066

On the day after Christmas, 1996, James E. Webb sat in the upstairs office of the General Wayne Inn, working on the books for the restaurant and hotel business he ran with his partner, Guy Sileo Jr. Business was not good. The two were having trouble paying their bills because revenue in the business was down, perhaps by over a half a million dollars from what they had projected for the year. The venture was in peril, but could the General Wayne Inn really be in serious trouble? It had been operating as a business in this location continuously since 1704, making it one of the longest-running commercial enterprises in the United States. It was a miracle that the three-story building even stood, this many years later. In its life, it had played host to the great and famous, people like George Washington and General Lafayette, Benjamin Franklin, Edgar Allan Poe, and General "Mad Anthony" Wayne, the man for whom it was named. Wayne had served his country well, including a major supporting role at Valley Forge with Washington. Countless others had passed through the inn, and many said that some had stayed, in the form of ghosts. Particularly noteworthy were the Hessians, mercenaries hired by the British to fight the colonists during the American Revolution, who were said to haunt the place centuries after they had died in the area.

As Webb studied the numbers for the inn, someone entered the office quietly and placed a gun against the back of his head. A moment later he was dead, from a single gunshot. His body fell backward onto the floor of the office. The small wound was almost undetectable but once the police realized the man had been shot, they focused their attention on the business partner. The two men had taken out life insurance policies on each other. If one of them died, the insurance proceeds would more than make up for the bad year suffered by the General Wayne Inn. The survivor could make a go of it as a sole proprietor.

The General Wayne Inn is without question the oldest murder house in America, even though the one documented murder that took place there happened in 1996. It is also the murder house with the most history to it, the kind of history that lends itself to ghost stories. The inn was built in 1704 in Merion, Pennsylvania, less than ten miles from Philadelphia. A colonist named Robert Jones built the inn on land he bought for twenty shillings. The man he bought the land from had gotten title to it from William Penn.

The first owner of the property named it the Wayside Inn, but it went through a series of name changes as time went by. After Jones died, the inn was run by a man named Anthony Tunis, and he named the inn Tunis Ordinary. At other times it was known as the William Penn Inn, for the original owner of the land, and Streeper's Tavern, for Abraham Streeper, who was the proprietor in 1776. Streeper left the inn in the hands of his wife while he went off and fought the British. During the Revolutionary War, while the owner was off fighting, the inn saw a bit of action of its own. The inn had many important visitors and even ended up in enemy hands for a bit. General Wayne stopped by, and George Washington and General Lafayette visited the inn the day after Wayne was there. Just a few days later, members of the Continental Congress stopped in as they fled the advancing British. Shortly after they left, the redcoats rode into town and occupied Streeper's Tavern. Skirmishes took place around the inn, and this is where some of the ghost stories originate: Some Hessian soldiers were said to have died there or nearby. As with many ghost stories, details of the deaths of the subjects are hard to nail down.

After the Revolutionary War ended, General Wayne spent some time fighting Native Americans in the Northwest Territory. After his time out west, he traveled back to Merion and stopped at the inn. It was 1795 and, while General Wayne was basking in the glow of his recent campaign successes, the proprietor decided to name the inn after Wayne.

General Wayne was born in 1745—forty-one years after the inn first opened—and fought in the American Revolution. His career was so illustrious that he is remembered today by many things that were named after him. Towns, forts, buildings, bridges—in some parts of the country the name is ubiquitous. There is Fort Wayne, Indiana, and an actual Fort Wayne in Detroit. Detroit itself is in Wayne County, which also contains the city of Wayne. There was even another General Wayne Inn, this one in New York, about a hundred miles from the one in Lower Merion. The New York one was younger, having been built in the 1780s, but by 2013 it was abandoned and slated for demolition.

Many people wonder if General Wayne was insane; after all, they called him "Mad Anthony." It turns out that the nickname was a reference to his famous temper. He notoriously got mad at people who were incompetent or who didn't follow orders.

The inn always appeared to be prosperous. Over the years it even housed a post office and a general store at one time or another, but its primary role was as a tavern and inn. In 1843, Edgar Allan Poe was said to have carved his initials in either a window or a windowsill at the inn.

The General Wayne Inn—or "the Wayne," as regulars called it—was still hugely successful in the twentieth century. Patrons packed the bar, and the restaurant was filled with customers and cigarette smoke. In 1970, a man named Barton Johnson bought it. People familiar with the story of the inn remember his ownership for two reasons. The inn was a moneymaker during the period, and Johnson loved to tell people the inn was haunted. By the late 1980s, the story was so well known that the television series *Unsolved Mysteries* ran an episode about it, trying to track down the ghost of a Hessian soldier. Later, the inn would appear on television again when *America's Most Wanted* would run a piece on the Webb murder.

In 1995, the General Wayne Inn was purchased by James E. Webb and Guy Sileo Jr. for a little under $1.3 million. They borrowed almost all of it from banks and used a $100,000 gift from Sileo's father as a down payment. Webb would be the executive chef and Sileo would be the sous chef. They hired a talented young chef named Felicia Moyse to work for them. Webb and Sileo had worked together before, running a successful restaurant nearby. When they bought it, the inn was known for hosting big-band dances and for its old-fashioned menu. They hoped they could update the menu and atmosphere of the General Wayne Inn. For some reason, the updated menu didn't translate into success at the General Wayne. The old-timers were scared off by the cutting-edge cuisine, and the younger crowd never got the message that the eighteenth-century inn was now a hip place to be seen.

The business began losing money almost instantly. The partners had spent money remodeling the building, and everything in it was pledged as collateral on the loan. Sales were decreasing steadily in 1996 and the restaurant was not going to survive. While Webb saw the writing on the wall, Sileo did not. The two argued about the direction the business was headed. Webb wanted to leave Sileo and the inn and to start his own restaurant. Sileo started drinking while at work and was engaged in a relationship with a young employee. Webb told Sileo he was going to leave the partnership after the holidays, and Sileo became violent. The two actually came to blows in the days leading up to the murder.

More troubling, Sileo approached Webb and demanded that Webb sign a statement that the $100,000 gift from Sileo's father had been a loan and not a gift. It was an odd request; previously, Sileo had given documentation to creditors that the money had been a gift. Why the change in heart? It is unclear if Webb knew it, but if the money was a gift, it could not be recovered in a bankruptcy proceeding. The bankruptcy estate would have had no assets on Christmas Day 1996—the inn was insolvent—but if one of the men died, there would be $650,000 in life insurance proceeds to scrap over. That's how it came to be that Webb was staring at accounting sheets filled with red ink when he was shot in the head.

The next morning after Webb was shot, the inn's pastry chef arrived for work and saw Webb's truck in the parking lot. Assuming that he was just doing office work, she went about her business. A few minutes later, Sileo arrived and the chef told him that Webb was in his office but that she had not spoken with him yet. Sileo went upstairs and returned shortly to tell her that Webb was dead in his office. The pastry chef went upstairs and looked at the body but thought it looked like he had just fallen backward and hit his head. Later that day, Sileo told Webb's wife that her husband had been "shot," even though everyone who had seen the body initially thought he had simply fallen and hit his head.

The police investigated, and at first their obvious suspect, Sileo, had an alibi. The young chef, Felicia Moyse, told investigators she was with Sileo at the time of the shooting. The police continued their investigation, looking for other possibilities. All evidence kept pointing back at Sileo. They discovered that Sileo owned a gun that was the same caliber as the murder weapon, but it was tested and it was not connected to the crime. Witnesses, however, told police that Sileo had said, "I really feel like I need to shoot someone," more than once, in recent weeks. A bartender from another restaurant that Sileo frequented told police that Sileo had once asked him about extradition laws and wondered if the bartender knew of any good countries to "hide out if you wanted to kill someone." Sileo had asked this just a month before Webb was killed.

A grand jury convened and Sileo was called to testify. There he swore that he owned only the one gun of that caliber and that he had not shot anyone with it. Later, a police wiretap caught Sileo telling someone he had, in fact, owned two guns of that caliber. Sileo was tried and convicted of perjury and false swearing. At that point, the state decided to prosecute Sileo for the murder of Webb.

The case had also provided other drama. One of the reasons that Sileo and Webb had fought was over the inappropriate relationship Sileo, who was married, was having with an employee of the inn. When he was first questioned by the police regarding his whereabouts on the night of the murder, Sileo said he was with Moyse, the young chef from the inn. As the investigation focused on Sileo, Moyse was Sileo's lifeline. On February 24, 1997, Moyse shot herself in the head with a handgun belonging to her father in her parents' bedroom. Moyse was Sileo's only alibi witness.

Sileo was prosecuted for the murder of Webb and on August 1, 2001, he was convicted of first-degree murder. During the trial it was revealed that when Webb was murdered, the life insurance company had paid the $650,000 from the policy taken on Webb's life in favor of the business. $433,303 of it was used to pay off a small business loan and the remainder was placed into escrow, where it became the subject of bankruptcy proceedings that Sileo had initiated shortly after Webb's murder. If the bankruptcy court had accepted the argument that the gift from Sileo's father had really been a loan, then some of the money from the life insurance proceeds could have been given to Sileo's father in repayment. Sileo filed a series of appeals, but they were denied by the higher courts in Pennsylvania.

The General Wayne Inn traded hands several times after Webb's death. In 1999, the building sold for almost $1,000,000, but the new buyer had to invest another $200,000 in renovations. The last restaurant venture on the site closed in 2002. Many people were starting to believe that the building was cursed, if not haunted. The last person to operate the General Wayne Inn as a restaurant was Frank Cacciutti, who had run a very successful restaurant before trying one at this location. Business was dismal. It wasn't until local papers ran stories that he was about to close that anyone showed up in any significant numbers. "We're extremely busy tonight," he told a reporter. "Everybody wants to watch the train wreck."

In 2003, an organization bought the property to convert it into the Chabad Center for Jewish Life. No longer operating as a restaurant, it became a place of education and outreach. Even though the local tax authority assessed the value of the inn at a million dollars, the selling price was reportedly $650,000. To convert it to its current use the organization invested more than a million dollars in the building, although the exterior was not altered. The building contains fourteen thousand square feet and still has a balcony on its second floor. Unlike the string of restaurants that had failed in the location, this enterprise is thriving. The name *General Wayne Inn* is still visible on the side of the building.

The building is privately owned. It can be seen from the road.

---

* "Was General 'Mad Anthony' Wayne Really Mad?" ushistory.org/paoli/history/waynemad.htm
* "General Wayne Inn in Merion to Close," *The (Philadelphia) Inquirer*, July 19, 2002.
* Chabad Center for Jewish Life at the General Wayne Inn, chabad.org/centers/default_cdo/aid/118357/jewish/Chabad-Center-for-Jewish-Life-at-the-General-Wayne-Inn.htm

The Ultimate Random Murder

ANDREW CUNANAN
KILLS GIANNI VERSACE

1997

1116 Ocean Drive
Miami Beach, Florida 33139

On the morning of July 15, 1997, fashion icon Gianni Versace walked three blocks south from his Miami Beach mansion to the News Café, a popular restaurant and newsstand, where he picked up some magazines. The walk along Ocean Drive is a pleasant one; on the opposite side of the street is Lummus Park and a public beach that sits between the ocean and ten or eleven blocks of trendy and busy establishments along the way. The fifty-year-old Versace then walked the short distance home a few minutes before 9:00 A.M. and paused to unlock the huge iron gates that opened into his estate. At that moment, Andrew Cunanan, a fugitive on a cross-country killing spree and the subject of a well-publicized nationwide manhunt, walked up behind him and shot him twice, in the neck and head.

Employees inside the home ran out when they heard the gunshots and found Versace lying lifeless on the front steps. They saw Cunanan running from the scene. A security camera trained on the gates had not been turned on at the time.

Cunanan fled. He ran to a parking garage a couple of blocks away, where he had left a truck he had stolen from an earlier murder victim. He quickly changed out of the clothes he had been wearing and dropped them on the ground next to the truck. When police canvassed the area, they found the clothing and identified the truck, linking Cunanan to Versace's killing. Later, police would be criticized for not spotting the truck earlier. It had been parked in the same spot, abandoned, for the two months that Cunanan had been hiding in Miami Beach before he killed Versace. Versace's murder left several unanswered questions: Why had Cunanan targeted him and how had police not caught Cunanan in the weeks leading up to Versace's murder?

Giovanni Versace was a rock star in the fashion world. Born in 1946, he founded a company that marketed clothing, accessories, fragrances, makeup, and even home furnishings. By the 1990s, he was a household name and often spent time with the ultrarich and famous. His fashion shows were among the hottest tickets with the elite. And, on July 15, 1997—at age fifty—he was shot to death by a stranger on the front steps of his mansion in Miami, one of the most expensive residences in North America.

Versace was born in Reggio Calabria, Italy, where he was first shown the world of fashion by his mother, who was a dressmaker. Although he helped her make dresses at times, he went to school to study architecture. Of the two vocations, it was fashion that called to him. He went to Milan to work in the fashion industry and founded his own fashion line. In 1978 he opened his first boutique, and by the 1990s his companies were making profits of $900 million annually.

As his wealth increased, he acquired large homes in the United States and Europe. He bought a huge home known as Casa Casuarina on Ocean Drive, in Miami Beach, in 1992. The house had been built in 1930 and was modeled after a home in the Dominican Republic, said to be the oldest house in this hemisphere. Christopher Columbus's family once lived in it; it was known as the Alcázar de Colón.

When the man who built Casa Casuarina in Miami Beach died, the next owner bought it in 1937; his name was Jacques Amsterdam and he called it the Amsterdam Palace. When Versace bought the Miami Beach version of the Alcázar de Colón, he expanded it. He invested another $33 million in furnishing, remodeling, and updating it. The result was even more opulent. At roughly twenty thousand square feet, it contained ten bedrooms and eleven bathrooms. He added a courtyard, another wing, and a swimming pool. The estate was huge; it covered one third of the block it sat on. It was also the only residence on that stretch of Ocean Drive. It was surrounded by a tall iron-and-concrete fence and wall, which were twelve feet tall at points. The front of the property was marked by a pair of iron gates that opened onto Ocean Drive. Versace split his time between this home and others he owned in Europe.

Andrew Phillip Cunanan was born in California in 1969. He was said to be of above-average intelligence, multilingual, charming, and openly gay. He grew up in an affluent family but his father, a stockbroker, ran into legal trouble and fled the country shortly after Andrew graduated from high school. Andrew began relying on older boyfriends for financial support. His rent, his car, and his living expenses were often paid by older gentlemen who were happy to pay them in exchange for dating Cunanan. He dropped out of college, worked as a gay prostitute in San Francisco, and became involved in making hard-core pornography, much of which was sadomasochistic in nature. He also tried breaking into Hollywood films. He auditioned for bit parts in movies and had no qualms about approaching famous people when he saw them at parties. Lisa Kudrow found herself cornered by Cunanan at a party, and Hugh Grant almost had Cunanan in one of his films, but the casting director passed on the unknown Cunanan.

In 1997, Cunanan became convinced he had acquired AIDS. He got himself tested but never returned to find out the results of the test. He was so overwhelmed with the belief that he had the disease that he didn't feel he needed to see the results. His mood changed, as did his behavior. He became depressed and starting using drugs. He gained weight and stopped worrying about his appearance. Cunanan had never been arrested before 1997 and had never appeared on the radar of law enforcement. That would soon change as he made his way onto the FBI's Ten Most Wanted list with a cross-country killing spree.

That year, he decided to visit a former boyfriend named Jeffrey Trail, who had moved to Minneapolis. While in Minnesota, Cunanan discovered that Trail was a friend of David Madson, another former boyfriend of Cunanan's who also now lived in Minneapolis. What were the odds? Cunanan became jealous. He may also have been upset that the two men had managed to escape the world where Cunanan felt trapped. He arranged to meet with Trail and Madson at Madson's apartment. An argument ensued and Cunanan began beating Madson with a hammer. Once he was dead, Trail helped Cunanan roll Madson's body into a carpet. Cunanan then shot and killed Trail. The police didn't have to work very hard to figure out who was behind the killings. They found Cunanan's backpack at Madson's apartment and a message from Cunanan on Trail's answering machine. Identifying the killer was easy; catching him became the hard part.

After shooting Trail, Cunanan fled Minnesota and traveled to Chicago. Within a few days, he had killed again. This time, the victim was a well-known real estate developer named Lee Miglin. It is unclear how Miglin and Cunanan crossed paths. There is no evidence that Cunanan knew Miglin or had ever met him before. Neighbors had seen Miglin earlier that day, and it is possible that Cunanan simply happened to pass by while looking for someone to rob. Cunanan tortured and killed Miglin, burglarized his house, and stole his car. With three murders in such a short time and in two different states, the FBI quickly placed Cunanan on their Ten Most Wanted list, and the media began broadcasting his likeness with descriptions of the crimes he was said to have committed. Cunanan fled the state in Miglin's car and headed east. In Pennsville, New Jersey, he decided to hide out in a cemetery. At this point, he had heard news reports on the radio and knew the police were looking for him. At the cemetery, he encountered and killed the caretaker, William Reese. He abandoned Miglin's car and stole Reese's truck. He headed to southern Florida. Again, police would be able to recreate Cunanan's steps quite easily. They canceled the alert regarding Miglin's car and issued a new one for the truck Cunanan had now stolen.

Despite the fact that he did little to hide his crimes, the police had a hard time catching Cunanan. He drove to Florida and checked into the Normandy Plaza Hotel at 6979 Collins Avenue in Miami Beach, after inquiring about monthly rates. He spent a couple of months in the Miami area and gave the police a golden opportunity to catch him. When he had killed Miglin, he had also stolen some rare coins from Miglin's house. To get spending money in Miami Beach, Cunanan decided to pawn one of the coins at a local shop called Cash on the Beach on July 7. The pawn shop followed the law and had Cunanan fill out a pawn slip for the coin he was pawning, and Cunanan filled it out with his actual name and the address of the hotel where he was staying. He showed the proprietor identification that showed his name was Andrew Cunanan. The shop gave him his money and he left. The shop then turned the pawn slip in to the Miami Beach Police Department, where the slip sat unnoticed in a pile of paperwork from July 8 until July 15. The delay had monumental consequences. July 15 was the same day Cunanan shot Versace.

When Gianni Versace was gunned down on the front steps of his mansion, Miami Beach police realized very quickly that Cunanan was the killer. But they could find no connection between the two men. It was a question that was never answered satisfactorily. It very well could be that Cunanan simply decided to kill someone famous before his killing spree ended. Others suggested that Cunanan may have met Versace someplace previously and felt slighted. While this theory is possible, it has never been verified by the police that the two ever met previously.

After shooting Versace, Cunanan did not run far. He found an unoccupied double-decker houseboat docked at Indian Creek, just a few miles from Versace's mansion, and broke into it. The boat was called *The New Year* and it was docked at 5250 Collins Avenue. Meanwhile, the police sent a SWAT team to the hotel where Cunanan had been staying and burst into the wrong room without realizing it. The room was vacant. It would be two more days before they realized their mistake and went back to search the room he had listed on the pawn receipt. No one was in that room either, but there was a pile of books Cunanan had checked out from the Miami Public Library, mostly on art.

Eight days after Versace had been killed, the caretaker of the houseboat at Indian Creek arrived to check on it. When he got aboard, he noticed that a door on the boat had been forced open. Carefully looking inside, he saw that someone was living in the boat. Then, he heard a gunshot. The caretaker called the police, who quickly came and surrounded the boat. A few hours later, with hundreds of law enforcement personnel swarming the dock, police entered and found Cunanan dead with a self-inflicted gunshot wound to the head. The gun he had shot himself with was identified as the murder weapon used to kill two of his victims and had been stolen from his first victim, Jeffrey Trail. News reports indicated that Cunanan had shot himself in the face. He was positively identified by a thumbprint.

Identifying the ownership of the houseboat Cunanan had moved into was confusing as well. Early news reports said it belonged to a man named Torsten Reineck, a fugitive from German law enforcement who was wanted for tax evasion. He owned the Apollo Spa in Las Vegas, which was well known in the gay community. It was unclear if Cunanan knew Reineck. Later news reports said the boat was actually owned by a man named Frank Matthias Ruehl.

In January 1998, the Miami Beach PD held what they called the "final" news conference on the Versace murder.

Newspapers called it "the biggest department case ever." The police noted that there were several possible explanations for why Cunanan had targeted Versace, but little evidence to support any of them. With Cunanan's death, the questions would remain unanswered. "We had a million questions we wanted to ask him," a Miami Beach PD representative told the press, referring to Cunanan. There were a million questions the public wanted to ask of the Miami Beach PD. Why hadn't they found Cunanan when the pawn slip was given to them? Why didn't anyone notice the stolen truck that sat abandoned for two months before Versace was killed? Several credible tips had been given to the police before the murder that Cunanan was in Miami Beach. Why hadn't the public been warned?

On July 24, a funeral for Gianni Versace was held in Milan, attended by many of his friends. Elton John and Sting sang a duet as part of the service. Princess Diana and Carolyn Kennedy were in attendance. Well-known members of the fashion universe such as Giorgio Armani, Karl Lagerfeld, and Naomi Campbell paid their respects.

The houseboat where Cunanan had hidden after the murder was in the news for a bit longer. *The New Year* suffered a mishap in December 1997. Its bilge pump became blocked by something and the boat partially sank into Indian Creek. When the owner, Ruehl, took no steps to repair or remove the boat, the city threatened to have it condemned. After sitting on the bottom of Indian Creek for a month, the partially submerged boat was demolished by the city at a cost of $16,000.

The Versace mansion on Ocean Drive remained empty for a few years after Versace's murder. Then a man named Peter Loftin bought the home in 2000 for a reported $19 million. He turned it into the Villa by Barton G Hotel and Restaurant; *Forbes* magazine called it a "high-end boutique hotel." Rooms started at around a thousand dollars a night and each one included a private butler. In 2012, the mansion was put up for sale with an asking price of $125 million, making it one of the two most expensive residential properties for sale in the United States at the time. With the real-estate listing, many of the home's finer details became more publicized. The pool, for example, is fifty-four feet long and lined with twenty-four-karat gold. The interior walls of the house are hand-painted with murals, and each room was individually designed by Versace.

By July 2013, the asking price of the mansion had been lowered to a mere $75 million, but still there were no takers. The holder of the mortgage began moving toward foreclosure, and that same month the owner of the home filed for Chapter 11 bankruptcy protection. Allegations and accusations flew between the parties. Meanwhile, the former business tenant—Villa by Barton G—had vacated. Eventually the mansion was sold at auction in September 2013. The sale price of $41.5 million was a far cry from the opening price of $125 million. Papers reported that Donald Trump had bid $41 million for the mansion but had been bested by an investor group that plans on reopening it as a hotel.

The mansion at 1116 Ocean Drive is privately owned but

visible from the street and sidewalk. There is a small barricade to keep people away from the gates and steps where Versace was murdered by Cunanan, and people still come by to get their photos taken in front of the home. Other than the address, there is nothing to indicate the notorious history of the property.

---

* Maureen Orth, "The Killer's Trail," *Vanity Fair*, September 1997.

America's Most Prolific Serial Killer

GARY RIDGWAY—THE GREEN RIVER KILLER

1998

21859 32nd Place
SeaTac, Washington 98198

In 1982, a young woman walking the streets of Seattle climbed into a pickup truck driven by a man who offered to pay her for sex. He drove her to his nearby home, where they had sex and then he strangled her. He dragged her body back out to his truck and drove to the nearby Green River, where he dumped her. The body would be found later with little evidence to point to a killer. Because the young woman was a runaway, possibly a prostitute, no one would notice her missing or be looking for her. The police would not know she existed until her body was found a week after she had been killed. The victim here, however, was simply a small piece of a much larger puzzle. Beginning in the early 1980s and continuing for almost two decades, Gary Ridgway would go on a killing spree of unprecedented scale, saying later that he may have killed eighty women before he was stopped. For a time during the 1980s, bodies of prostitutes and runaways were sometimes found on a weekly basis even as a task force combed through thousands of tips. Ridgway, nicknamed "The Green River Killer" after where some of his first victims were dumped, became the country's most prolific serial killer, and for many years the local police department appeared to be completely at a loss as to how to stop the killer in their area.

Gary Ridgway was born in 1949 and joined the navy as a young man. He spent time serving on a ship off the shore of Vietnam while he had a wife back in the states. This marriage would end and Ridgway would eventually marry two more times. His relationships with women were troubled, to put it mildly. He began seeing prostitutes, probably while in the navy, but continued long after returning to civilian life. He moved to Seattle and began working at a plant that built trucks, where he got a job working in a paint booth.

In January 1982, Ridgway bought a house in SeaTac, Washington, a suburb of Seattle. Around this time, a sixteen-year-old runaway named Wendy Lee Coffield was strangled, and her body was dumped in the Green River. A week later, some boys riding their bicycles across a bridge over the river looked down and spotted Coffield's body floating in the river. They thought it was a mannequin and went down to investigate. When they realized it was a real body, they called police. Coffield would be the first of a string of victims, with Ridgway killing so often that his victims were often not found in the order they were killed, or sometimes were found in groups because he dumped more than one body in the same spot. He killed his second victim in the woods and left her there, where she would not be found for two months. His third victim was murdered on July 25 but not discovered until August 12, 1982. She was also found floating in the Green River. The three bodies were of women who had been strangled after being picked up on the streets of Seattle. If the police were not sure yet they had a serial killer on the loose, it would become painfully clear on August 15, 1982. A man rafting down the Green River found the body of a woman floating in the river. Shocked, he noticed another woman's body just under the surface at the same spot. He went ashore and asked someone to call the police. When they arrived, they searched the area and found a third victim, another young woman who had been strangled, not far from the river.

From this point forward, bodies of strangled prostitutes and runaways would be discovered scattered all over the area in an alarming number. Amazingly, Ridgway was known to the police during this time but only as a customer of prostitutes. He was arrested in April 1982, and again that May, for soliciting prostitution. Investigators did not link him to the killings. Over that summer, more women disappeared from the streets of Seattle, many of them last seen in the area where Ridgway was arrested. The area was well known as a place for prostitution and Ridgway was just one of many johns arrested in that area. Meanwhile, victims began turning up on a weekly basis.

Despite the close calls, Ridgway continued picking up women and killing them, many of whom he brought to his house in SeaTac. Other times he would kill them in a secluded spot, outdoors, or while parked in his truck. Ridgway would then find an out of the way place to dump the victim's body. Some locations he used more than once. Tips and leads flooded in but had the wrong effect; authorities appeared overwhelmed by the information and seemingly got nowhere. One confusing aspect of the crime wave was that the victims were not always discovered immediately. A series of women would disappear over a stretch of time without any bodies being found. Then someone would stumble upon a stash of victims' bodies and notify the police.

The bodies were also revealing very little information to investigators. DNA testing was still being developed, and little else was found at the sites where the bodies were found. Investigators found small amounts of body fluid that might have come from the killer, but otherwise they had little to go on.

In 1982, the Green River Killer struck at least sixteen times. He killed twenty-four more times in 1983. Then he killed twice more in 1984 and stopped. Police were not sure at first, since bodies continued to be found. They formed a task force to work on the cases to date—authorities had identified only sixteen bodies they considered victims of the killer—

although Ridgway had already killed more than three dozen. The task force combed through mountains of clues and tips, and Ridgway finally turned up on their radar. He was known to frequent the areas where the victims were last seen and had been arrested for soliciting prostitution. He was given a polygraph and the operator of the test concluded that Ridgway was being truthful when he denied any connection to the killings. Ridgway was released.

In February 1985, Ridgway attended a singles event at a local bar and met a woman named Judith who was recently divorced after a marriage of almost two decades. Ridgway impressed her with what a gentleman he could be. He helped her with her chair when sitting down at a table; he opened doors for her. She later said that he made her smile every day. Unbeknownst to her, Ridgway had killed at least forty-two women by this time but had not killed anyone since March 1984. There were some odd things about him, though. When she first visited his house in SeaTac, the carpeting had recently been torn up and removed, and he was sleeping on a mattress and box spring that were lying on the floor. He told her that the carpeting had been damaged by the previous tenants of the house and that an ex-girlfriend had demanded her bed back after a breakup. Judith decided to overlook the shoddy décor. In later years, she would learn that he had removed the carpeting and the bed in an attempt to destroy evidence at a crime scene.

Ridgway did not kill any women for the entire first year he

dated Judith. But then he started coming home late and leaving for work early. He told her it was work related, union meetings he had to attend and so on. Again, since he treated her so well, she decided to believe him. The two were married in 1988. Ridgway did not kill anyone that year or the next. But he couldn't help himself and began killing again in 1990 and again in 1998. The number of victims and the frequency with which he killed them had clearly been slowed, but authorities knew that the Green River Killer was alive and well.

In 1987, the police had again taken a look at Ridgway. This time they took hair and DNA samples from him. It still took the police several years to find DNA evidence on a victim that could be matched to a killer, partially because advancements in DNA had not progressed enough yet. But when a match was finally made, it pointed to Ridgway. He was arrested on November 30, 2001, and charged with several murders. Once the investigators found out that Ridgway worked in a factory painting trucks, they went back through their evidence samples and found microscopic traces of paint that could be conclusively linked to the specific brand and type of paint Ridgway worked with at the time. Even more murder charges were leveled against him. And authorities were certain they had caught their man.

Ridgway maintained his innocence at first while prosecutors indicated they would seek the death penalty. After a year or so, Ridgway agreed to cooperate with the authorities in exchange for the dropping of the death penalty from the possible outcomes of his case. His bargaining chip? He would help authorities locate the remains of other victims and also gave details for each so their cases could be closed. At the time the bargain was struck, the police only had evidence tying Ridgway to seven victims. He agreed to confess to a total of forty-eight victims, meaning that the police could close another forty-one cases with his cooperation.

Ridgway pleaded guilty to forty-eight counts of murder in exchange for getting prison time instead of the death penalty. Authorities actually took Ridgway in a van and drove him around as he pointed out places where he had left victims' bodies. The court sentenced him to forty-eight consecutive life sentences. In case anyone wondered what would drive someone to kill so many people, Ridgway told the court:

> *I picked prostitutes because I hate most prostitutes and I did not want to pay them for sex. I also picked prostitutes as victims because they were easy to pick up without being noticed. I knew they would not be reported missing right away and might never be reported missing. I picked prostitutes because I thought I could kill as many of them as I wanted without getting caught.*

In December 2010, another victim was found who had not been among the forty-eight victims Ridgway had confessed to earlier. The prosecutors filed charges and Ridgway pleaded guilty to a forty-ninth murder charge. The judge added a forty-ninth life sentence to the end of his already impossibly long sentence. In his discussions with police, Ridgway admitted killing as many as seventy-one women in all. Later, investigators wondered about the lie detector test Ridgway had passed. The "charts" created by the polygrapher were still in the file, and when they were examined by other polygraph experts, it was determined that Ridgway should have been deemed to have failed the test. The results had simply been misinterpreted.

Ridgway's wife initially believed that her husband was innocent. She visited him in jail and later spoke of how hard it was to be separated from the man she loved. Eventually, as she became aware of the strength of the case against him, she came to realize that he had led a double life and that he was, indeed, the Green River Killer. She filed for divorce and later cooperated with an author who wrote a book about her experience: *Green River Serial Killer—Biography of an Unsuspecting Wife*. As the years passed, Ridgway acknowledged that his estimates for how many women he killed had been low. He later said the number may have been as high as eighty. Investigators continued looking for the remains of his victims but have not found any more in recent years, even though Ridgway continues to give them details of where he dumped victims. Now, some think he may be leading investigators on a wild-goose chase.

The house where Ridgway lived when he killed most of his

victims and, according to his own statements, where he committed many of the murders is still standing on 32nd Place in SeaTac. Before she moved out of it, Judith told of how the house became a focal point of rage; people would come by and vandalize it, presumably because they couldn't get to Ridgway and harm him instead. The house is small, at 1,150 square feet, and was built in about 1970. It has three bedrooms and one bath and is on a fairly small lot. The last time it changed hands was in 1999 when it sold for a little over $112,000. It is privately owned.

---

* Matthew Preusch, "Washington: Seeking Death Sentence in Killings," *New York Times*, April 16, 2002.

Postpartum Depression on Trial

ANDREA YATES

2001

942 Beachcomber Lane
Houston, Texas 77062

On June 20, 2001, Russell Yates went to his job at NASA, believing that his mother would arrive soon at his house to help his wife, Andrea, with the five Yates children. The youngest was six months old and Andrea had recently been having trouble coping with the children. Worse, she had been suffering from mental illness and had recently gone off her medication. Russell's mother did not arrive in time. Andrea filled the bathtub with water and drowned her children in it, one at a time. She started with the youngest. After she drowned each child, she would place the child's body in her bed. When she had finished drowning the last child, she phoned the police and said, "I just killed my kids." It was 9:48 A.M. She then called her husband and kept saying, "It's time, it's time," over and over again to him. Russell didn't understand what she was trying to tell him and asked her if someone was hurt. She told him that the kids were hurt. He asked her which of the children, and she replied, "All of them."

Russell raced the three miles home and found his house surrounded by police cars and ambulances. The police wouldn't let him into the house, but he quickly figured out what had happened. He sat on the front lawn and tried to process it. Moments earlier, the police had arrived and had been met by a calm Andrea. Her hair and clothing were wet and she casually told them that she had killed her children. She told them that there were four in her bed and another was still in the bathtub. Detectives had never seen anything like it—five dead children and their mother nonchalantly telling them how she had just killed them all. When they asked her why, she said, "Because I'm a bad mother." It was one of the most troubling murder cases in recent history. The story of the murders made national headlines, and the trials that followed brought postpartum mental illness into the national conversation as well.

Andrea Kennedy was born in Houston in 1964 and by all standards was a very bright person. She was a good student, graduating from high school as valedictorian, and she studied nursing at both the University of Houston and the University of Texas. In 1986, she began working as a nurse, and three years later she met Russell Yates. Yates was an engineer who would eventually work at NASA. They married in 1993 and over the next few years they had five children: four sons and one daughter. In 2001, they ranged in age from six months to seven years old.

Before meeting Andrea, Russell had befriended a street preacher named Michael Peter Woroniecki he had met at Auburn University. Woroniecki was eccentric: He began his ministry standing on street corners in Grand Rapids, Michigan, preaching the Gospel with a bullhorn. The people of Grand Rapids found his loud public sermons obnoxious, and he was arrested several times as a result. He reportedly struck a deal with local authorities after his last arrest there: He promised to leave town and preach elsewhere if the charges against him were dropped.

Woroniecki set out to spread the Gospel around the world. He drove across Europe in a van and exhorted listeners at every stop to follow Jesus. He often stationed himself in large cities and capitals, preaching fire and brimstone. He spent a lot of time in the United States too. He claimed to have preached God's word in all fifty states and was often seen at sporting events or places where large numbers of people congregated, such as the 1996 Atlanta Olympics. When Russell first met Woroniecki, he had gotten some religious literature from the preacher and began corresponding with him about the Bible. Russell had even begun emulating some aspects of the preacher's itinerant lifestyle. When he and Andrea had been married a couple of years, Russell insisted that the young couple should live simply, and they moved into a recreational vehicle in a trailer park rather than a house.

Russell introduced his wife to the preacher, and she seemed to like his message as well. In 1998, Andrea and Russell went to Miami to visit with Woroniecki. On that trip, they bought the motorhome the preacher had been using in his travels, a 1978 GMC bus that had been converted into an RV. Russell and Andrea returned to Texas with the vehicle and used it to replace the recreational vehicle in which they had been living. Andrea would soon appear to be as influenced by Woroniecki's philosophies as her husband had been.

In 1999, after their fourth child was born, Andrea began hallucinating and hearing voices when no one else was around. She attempted suicide, taking an overdose of antidepressants that had been prescribed to her father. She was admitted to a psychiatric hospital and spent almost a week there before being released. She then began regularly seeing a psychiatrist. Less than a month later, Russell found Andrea in the bathroom, holding a knife to her neck. She was admitted to a hospital again. There, she told a doctor she had been having visions and hearing voices ever since the birth of her fourth child, Luke. Her psychiatrist would later say that Andrea was one of the "five sickest" patients she had ever treated and said that much of her illness was caused by postpartum issues. Her psychiatrist warned her—and Russell—that Andrea should not have any more children because of the high risk of a postpartum psychotic episode. It was advice the couple would ignore.

While Andrea was in the hospital, Russell decided it was time for them to move from the bus into a real home. He bought a house on Beachcomber Lane in Houston. Meanwhile, Russell was working for NASA at the Lyndon B. Johnson Space Center in Houston. Their new home was only three miles from where he worked, giving him just a five-minute commute. In November 2000, Andrea gave birth to Mary, their fifth child. Shortly before she became pregnant, Andrea had stopped taking her medication.

Andrea's mental illness grew worse. She continued suffering from postpartum depression and psychosis. She was hospitalized again in March 2001 but was discharged after two weeks when Russell and Andrea asked for her to be released. Andrea's doctor specifically warned Russell to not leave her alone with their children. One of the problems, however, was that the couple had decided to homeschool their five children. The children were home all day long with Andrea while Russell worked. And people would later note that Andrea appeared to be overwhelmed by her household and teaching responsibilities. As a result, what few visitors they had often observed that the house was a mess and that Andrea was struggling with even the most basic chores.

Because of the perceived dangers in leaving Andrea home alone with the children, Russell arranged for his mother to come to Houston and help Andrea. Russell's mother did not live with them in the house but stayed at a hotel nearby. She would come over after Russell left for work and then return to her hotel in the evening. While helping Andrea around the house she witnessed Andrea's odd behavior. Andrea was often silent and nonresponsive to her mother-in-law. She didn't eat and she would scratch at her head until she had bald spots. Sometimes, she would stare into space and go silent, or just talk to herself. Once, she filled the bathtub with water and then simply left it standing. When her mother-in-law asked her why she had done that, Andrea said she had filled the tub "in case I need it," without any further explanation. At the time it seemed odd but not terribly frightening.

Russell had Andrea readmitted to the psychiatric hospital when it became apparent that her mental state was not getting better. This time, she was prescribed Haldol—an antipsychotic drug sometimes used to treat schizophrenia—and her doctors even recommended electroconvulsive (sometimes called electroshock) therapy. She agreed to take the drugs but declined the therapy. After ten days, she was sent home again. Russell's mother noticed a slight improvement in Andrea, but she still seemed distant and emotionless. After a visit to her doctor at which she claimed she was not feeling suicidal and denied having psychotic thoughts, her medication was reduced. This visit was on June 18, 2001. She killed all of her children on the twentieth.

A ndrea Yates was charged with three counts of murder; the prosecutors decided to "save" the two other murder charges so they could retry her if she somehow was found not guilty for these three murders. It became much more complicated than anyone would have expected for a case where the defendant admitted she had killed her children. Her attorneys argued that she was obviously insane. They said Yates suffered from postpartum depression, which resulted in a mental state whereby she did not know right from wrong. Meanwhile, the prosecution felt they had a good chance of proving that she had known what she was doing when she drowned her children. Yates had admitted to waiting for her husband to leave for work before she acted. She had locked up the dog, which normally had the run of the house. And while she had been treated for a variety of depressive-type illnesses, she had been discharged from the hospital. Her doctor had even discontinued her medication, apparently in the belief that she was healthy.

The prosecution pointed out that Yates had even explained why she had killed her children. "My children were not righteous," she had told them. "I let them stumble. They were doomed to perish in the fires of hell." Some people wondered if Andrea's religious statements indicated an unnatural fascination with the teachings of Woroniecki, the fire-and-brimstone street preacher. If so, the actions might have had nothing to do with mental illness but more to do with religious zealotry.

Regarding the insanity defense, Texas followed the rule used in many states: The defendant had to be incapable of telling right from wrong at the time of the killings to not be held accountable for them. To the surprise of many observers, Russell decided to support and defend his wife, the woman who admitted drowning their five children. He held a press conference and showed reporters a family portrait from happier times. He explained his belief that Andrea was mentally ill and not responsible for what she had done. "She wasn't in the right frame of mind," he said.

The first problem the defense attorneys ran into was Andrea. She would not cooperate with her own attorneys. She told one that she did not want to plead not guilty. The attorneys wondered if she was competent to stand trial when she told them that Satan was talking to her in her jail cell. The attorneys asked the court to hold a hearing on whether Andrea was even fit for trial. The competency exam was set to begin on September 11, 2001. When news of the 9/11 attacks reached the courthouse, the hearing was postponed. Eventually, the hearing was reconvened and the court listened to expert testimony and concluded that Andrea was competent to stand trial for murder regardless of whose voice she heard talking to her when she was alone in her cell.

At her trial, both sides presented expert testimony, and by the time it was over, ten psychiatrists and two psychologists had testified. One of them was an overzealous expert for the prosecution who would undo their case, but not before he had created some drama on the witness stand. Dr. Park Dietz testified that not only did Yates know what she was doing at the time of the killings, she had seen a television show with a similar theme and then had simply mimicked the episode in an apparently effort to play insane. Dietz said Yates had acted out an episode of the television show *Law & Order*. It seemed to make sense that Dietz would know; he had been a consultant for the show. That episode, according to Dietz, involved a woman who had drowned her children and then escaped liability by pleading insanity. He testified, under oath:

> As a matter of fact, there was a show of a woman with postpartum depression who drowned her children in the bathtub and was found insane and it was aired shortly before the crime occurred.

The prosecutor found witnesses who confirmed that Andrea did, indeed, watch *Law & Order*.

The prosecution team argued the *Law & Order* angle as well. The prosecutor cross-examined one of Andrea's experts by asking:

> Did you know that in the weeks before June 20, there was a Law & Order *episode where a woman killed her children by drowning them in a bathtub, was defended on the basis of whether she was sane or insane under the law, and the diagnosis was post-*

partum depression and in the program the person
was found insane, not guilty by reason of insanity?
Did you know that?

The defense expert witness was caught unaware and admitted that he did not know about the episode. In the closing argument the prosecutor said, "These thoughts came to her, and she watches *Law & Order* regularly, she sees this program. There is a way out. She tells that to Dr. Dietz. A way out." The jury found Yates guilty after three and a half hours of deliberation. At the time of the trial and the verdict, many media reports recounted the tale of how Yates had mimicked actions she had seen on TV, believing it to be a good way to fake insanity.

A writer covering the trial for *Oprah* magazine had previously worked on the show *Law & Order* and didn't recall any episode of the show that mirrored the case of Andrea Yates. Word was passed to the defense and it was confirmed: There was no such episode. Defense counsel met with the prosecutors and noted that the key prosecution witness had testified falsely. He had also been the only witness who claimed that Andrea knew right from wrong when she killed her children. His testimony had clearly been vital to the prosecution's case. And now, it was apparent that it was deeply flawed. The prosecution argued that the matter of the false testimony wasn't all that important. Yates's attorneys argued to the trial court that this was grounds for a new trial, but the trial court denied the request. The court did not think the false testimony had been enough to influence the verdict. The judge did, however, tell the jury of Dietz's false testimony so they could take it into account during the punishment phase they were then asked to rule on. The same jury that found her guilty was then asked if Andrea was a continuing threat to society. If she was, she could be sentenced to death. They deliberated on this issue for only forty minutes and apparently concluded she was not a continuing threat to society. Yates was sent to prison for life. She would be eligible for parole in forty years.

Andrea's attorneys went to the Texas Court of Appeals, complained about the false testimony of Dietz, and asked for a new trial. The appeals court noted that Dietz had been the only mental health expert who had argued that Andrea knew right from wrong when she killed her children. If his testimony was suspect, the entire case of the prosecution went out the window. And so it did. The Texas Court of Appeals ordered a new trial for Yates.

The second time around, in July 2006, Yates was found not guilty by reason of insanity by a Texas jury. For his part, Park Dietz later claimed that his testimony regarding the nonexistent *Law & Order* episode was "an honest mistake" resulting from "human error." It seemed odd to many court observers that a consultant for a television show would accidentally come to believe that an episode of that show so closely resembled the case he was working on, when no such show existed. How closely did he consult on the show? And where did the notion even come from in the first place?

Russell Yates defended his wife at first, but eventually he filed for divorce. Later, he remarried. His second marriage took place just a few days before Andrea's second murder trial began and was held in the same church where the funerals for the children had been held. Some people questioned the timing of the wedding, but Russell told the Associated Press that Andrea was aware of his plans and that he and Andrea wished each other well.

Andrea is still in the custody of the state of Texas and is receiving treatment for mental illness. Her current attorney is working to see if she can be released back into society now that she has been treated for ten years. He believes she could gradually rejoin society and be fine. It is just unclear when, or if, the state of Texas would be willing to allow that.

Meanwhile, art imitates life. In 2004, a *Law & Order* episode titled "Magnificat" had a story line that appeared to be inspired by the Yates murders. In it, a severely depressed woman kills her children. However, this episode was shot well after Dietz had given the false testimony about the existence of such a show.

The Yates home was built in 1968. It was placed on the market in 2004 while awaiting the ruling from the Court of Appeals after the first trial. It was on the market for six months, listed at $109,900. According to listings, it is

1,620 square feet with three beds and two baths and sits on an 11,389-square-foot lot. The home is privately owned.

---

* Andrew Cohen, "10 Years Later, the Tragedy of Andrea Yates," *The Atlantic*, March 11, 2012.

Mob Hit in the Victorian Mansion

THE KREISCHER MANSION

2005

4500 Arthur Kill Road
Staten Island, New York 10309

Robert McKelvey spent time with some shady characters on Staten Island. Some of them were reputedly involved in organized crime, and the police had their suspicions about McKelvey as well. His business associates may have had mob connections and were the sort of people no one liked to talk about. One day, McKelvey was invited by Joseph Young, one of his associates, to the Kreischer Mansion, a three-story Victorian house that sat on top of a hill on Staten Island. Young was reputed to be an enforcer for a local crime organization. At least, that was what many people in the neighborhood thought. Certainly McKelvey knew it. But he headed over to talk to Young. McKelvey owed money to some very powerful people, according to law enforcement officials, and had recently angered some of them by mouthing off to the wrong people. Unbeknownst to McKelvey, the people he owed money to had decided they wouldn't mind writing the debt off—so long as McKelvey was dead.

The Kreischer Mansion looked like it had been built to order for a horror movie. It was surrounded by a tall wrought-iron fence, and the highlight of its façade was a turret. It was painted an odd combination of dark orange and green with maroon accents. Visitors to the house over the years had claimed it was haunted. Now, the only resident of the house was Young, an ex-Marine who had been hired as caretaker of the property and lived upstairs in the old place. We do not know what McKelvey was told to get him to the Kreischer Mansion. Perhaps Young just said they needed to talk. Or maybe he said he had a business proposition to discuss.

During the visit on March 29, 2005, according to prosecutors, Young attacked McKelvey and tried strangling him. McKelvey got away from Young and tried fleeing. Young chased after him and the two struggled. McKelvey put up a fight, so Young pulled a knife and stabbed him repeatedly. To make sure McKelvey was dead, Young dragged his body over to a pond on the property and held his head under water. He then hauled McKelvey's body into the mansion, called some of his business associates, and asked for help in disposing of the body.

Shortly after Young made the call, four other men arrived. They used hacksaws to chop up McKelvey's body and threw it into the old home's furnace. They cleaned up after themselves and went on with their lives. Not long after, the furnace was replaced, guaranteeing that the crime would be almost impossible to solve. McKelvey's sister filed a missing-person report, but the police had no leads and no idea where to begin looking. Considering the company McKelvey kept, the police weren't exactly inspired to go out and do a whole lot of looking without more to go on. It would take a police informant's tip to let the police know of McKelvey's grisly end.

The police would eventually arrest Young and four of his associates and charge them with the murder of McKelvey. The prosecution would later theorize that Young had been paid $8,000 to carry out the hit on McKelvey, which had been ordered because McKelvey had upset other members of the organization. The story had unraveled when one of the men who had helped chop up the body decided to tell the police what he knew and agreed to testify.

In 2008 Young was convicted of the murder along with a few other crimes—arson, armed robbery, gun smuggling— and sentenced to life in prison. News reports of the crime and the trial almost always highlighted the Kreischer Mansion, the setting of the murder. Despite its spooky exterior and the infamous murder that had taken place, the home had a remarkable history long before anyone was murdered there.

The Kreischer Mansion was built in 1885 and is Victorian in style. It is about 6,700 square feet and is one of several mansions built by a wealthy family that had made its money with a brick business. Balthasar Kreischer came to America from Bavaria, and in 1855 he established the Kreischer Brickworks. His business would flourish as he supplied bricks, made from clay located on Staten Island, to a booming building trade in New York City and the East Coast. He built housing for his workers and soon oversaw the factory town of Kreischerville. As his empire grew, so did his family. He built a mansion for himself and then a pair of mansions, one each for his two oldest sons, George and Edward. The company became B. Kreischer & Sons Fire Brick Manufactory. A certain amount of bad luck followed the family. Twice, the family's brick factory burned to the ground. The employees, however, were said to have fond feelings toward the family. On one occasion, the Kreischers furnished their employees—out of work while the factory was being rebuilt—with thousands of dollars of relief despite having no legal obligation to do so.

Shortly after the homes for his sons were finished, Balthasar died. Although the brick business continued after their father's death, it was never as successful as when their father was alive.

In 1895, Edward Kreischer committed suicide. No one knew why. The *New York Times* reported that he had been in good spirits shortly before he was found with a single bullet wound to his head and a gun lying next to his body, not far from the factory. Some people speculated that it was work related because his family life seemed fine.

One of the two mansions also burned down in the early twentieth century. The brick business ran until 1927. During World War I, at a time of anti-German sentiment, the name Kreischerville raised eyebrows. The locals began calling the town Charleston, perhaps after Charles Kreischer, Balthasar's son, who, despite his German last name, was still well liked in the community.

The remaining home, now simply called the Kreischer Mansion, has fourteen rooms—including five bedrooms and five baths—and was briefly used as a restaurant. It sits on a hill with a full acre of property in the area known as the Charleston neighborhood of Staten Island. Its address is on Arthur Kill Road—for the curious, "Kill" in this context is the Dutch word for "creek"—at the juncture with Kreischer Street. Stories abound on the Internet that the home is haunted. Among the spectral occupants is said to be the wife of Edward, the son who had killed himself. Some say she can be heard crying in the mansion, although this would seem a bit odd. She and her husband had lived in the other mansion, which is no longer standing.

It has been a while since the home was occupied as a residence. In 1996, it was converted into a restaurant. After the restaurant failed, the mansion was bought by Isaac Yomtovian, the man who hired Young as a caretaker while the home was being refurbished. Yomtovian paid $1,400,000 for the property in 2000 and invested another million dollars restoring the property in the next few years. When he bought it, the mansion's roof was caving in and everything down to and including the foundation needed work. Yomtovian tried to turn the property into an "active-adult community," but he couldn't secure financing for the project. At that point, Yomtovian decided to place the Kreischer Mansion on the market. The property now included five acres of surrounding land, and the initial asking price was $11.6 million. When he listed it for sale, he asked $1.6 million for the Kreischer Mansion and another $10 million for the surrounding acreage. The mansion itself had been listed previously for $2,499,000, which was then reduced to $1,599,000, but Yomtovian found no buyers. The real estate professionals suggested it would make a good spa or bed and breakfast. The surrounding property will almost certainly be developed. It is just a question of whether the Kreischer Mansion will be saved and to what use it will be put.

Yomtovian did tell a newspaper reporter that he had written a movie treatment about the mansion that, if made, would leave audiences spellbound. He also allowed producers of the show *Boardwalk Empire* to use the property in filming their pilot in 2009.

---

* William K. Rashbaum, "Grisly Mob Killing at S.I. Mansion Is Detailed," *New York Times*, May 12, 2006.

* "Conviction in Mob Murder at Staten Island's Kreischer Mansion," *Staten Island (NY) Advance*, October 27, 2008.

The Murder House
Where No One Was Murdered

THE GARDETTE-LAPRETE HOUSE

716 Dauphine Street
New Orleans, Louisiana 70116

In 1792, a mysterious stranger sailed into New Orleans and boldly asked to rent the most expensive home in the city. Money was no object and he—along with a large retinue—was soon ensconced in the Gardette-LaPrete House on Dauphine Street in the French Quarter. The stranger came from the Far East and was rumored to be a Turkish sultan—or the brother of the sultan—but few details emerged as to his identity. No one knew his name, and few cared. He was rich and spent his unending supply of money lavishly. Once the lease was signed, he moved into the huge home with his entourage, which included a harem, servants, eunuchs, and an abundance of opulent furniture, artwork, and other treasures befitting royalty. After moving in, the sultan beefed up security on the house, placing bars over the windows. Members of the sultan's staff patrolled outside the home. Some people began referring to the home as "The Sultan's Palace."

Then the sultan began throwing wild parties. At least, that was what it sounded like. He didn't invite his neighbors; he had more than enough people in his entourage to entertain without bringing strangers into the home. Loud music coming from the house could be heard on the street, and people walking by could smell exotic incense in the air.

One night the hard-partying sultan appeared to be outdoing his previous festivities. Neighbors were said to recall having heard yelling and screaming from the mansion but had thought little of it. By this time, they had gotten used to their boisterous neighbors from the Orient. The next morning, all was quiet on Dauphine Street. Even the guards were gone from in front of the house. Some curious neighbors investigated and found the front gate unlocked. Then they noticed what looked like blood seeping from under the front door. Some said the blood flowing under the front door was so copious, it had been spotted by a neighbor from across the street.

The police were summoned and the front door was quickly forced open, revealing a gruesome scene. It appeared that the inhabitants of the home had all been brutally murdered. Eunuchs, servant girls, and the rest of the sultan's entourage were all hacked to death, scattered about the huge mansion. Blood was everywhere, the home had been ransacked, and valuable artwork had vanished. The sultan was also missing.

Had he fled? Investigators tried to make sense of the scene when one of them noticed a man's hand reaching up from the soil in the courtyard. It was the sultan's; he had been buried alive.

Various theories were floated as to who had committed the brutal mass murder. A pirate ship was said to have been docked in the harbor around the time. Might the stories of the sultan's opulent lifestyle have reached the ears of men who would come to steal his treasure? Some wondered if the sultan was really a sultan after all. If he had been the brother of the sultan, perhaps his brother—the real sultan—had been angered by his brother and had sent assassins to kill him. Perhaps he had stolen the treasures—and the women—he had brought to New Orleans. Had his brother learned the whereabouts of the missing loot—and the missing women—and sought revenge and the recovery of the wealth? The crime was never solved.

The story of the Sultan's Palace is well known in New Orleans, and the home—which still stands—is one of the city's most infamous landmarks. What is commonly known as the Gardette-LaPrete House is within just a few blocks of the LaLaurie mansion and is also in the French Quarter. Anyone doing even the slightest amount of research on this story will immediately spot problems with it. The Gardette-LaPrete house was built in 1836 and named for its first two owners: the man who built it and the man who bought the Greek Revival home from him in 1839. The story of the house—and the murders said to have occurred there—is long and winding. Among other things, the second owner's name was Lepretre—one word—and no one was ever murdered in the house. Notwithstanding the facts, it is widely said that the "LaPrete" house was the site of a fantastical murder. That story has morphed through the years, to the point where it is highly unlikely that it will ever be extinguished.

The truth is not as spectacular as the story of the Sultan's Palace. In the late 1830s, Joseph Coulon Gardette built a three-and-a-half-story house on a piece of property he bought for four thousand piastres, an archaic unit of currency that probably corresponded with the equivalent of Spanish dollars, sometimes known as "pieces of eight." The stuccoed brick building was said to be the first home in New Orleans to have a basement. It fronted on Dauphine at the corner of Orleans and was quite large. Its front to Dauphine was almost 80 feet long, while another side stretched 33 feet on Orleans. The lot comprised 2,508 square feet. Because legal documents were filed with the local government—and survive to this day—we know details about the home's construction we might not know otherwise about so old a structure. The plans for the home were contained in the legal filings before construction began.

> The plinths of the ground floor and of the first story
> shall be panelled, the door and the window casing
> pilastered [sic], the doors with panels and movable
> blinds, the floors shall be made with planks six to

seven inches wide and one and one-quarter inch in thickness, the stairs shall have a mahogany handrail and mahogany balusters.

The entire construction project was slated to cost 14,500 piastres.

One of the most obvious features of the house is cast-iron work on the second- and third-floor balconies, which is often associated with the older homes in the French Quarter. It appears that this ironwork was added later. Architectural historians note that the ironwork on the balconies was not mentioned in the building plans, despite the high level of detail in the plans otherwise.

Gardette sold the home only a few years later to Jean Baptiste Lepretre, a wealthy man who lived on a plantation and intended the mansion to be a second home. Over the years, Lepretre's name would commonly be rendered as Le Prete or LaPrete. The selling price in 1839 was reportedly a little over $20,000. In later years, Lepretre would rent the house to others. Some said he had fallen on hard times, but others claimed that he simply had not been using the home enough to justify letting it sit vacant. Despite how much we know about the house's history and construction, almost nothing is certain about the murders that were said to have taken place there. How many people died? What were their names? Facts like these are hard to come by, and there are several variations on the story.

Researchers trying to learn more—such as the date of the crime or the names of the victims—encounter a huge gap in the evidence. There is no record of these events in local newspapers. Some modern writers suggest that the local authorities destroyed the records of the event, like the police reports, but how would they keep such a story out of the newspapers?

Deconstructing legends and myths can be difficult, particularly when they are not based on actual events. And the murders at the Gardette-LaPrete house never happened. This story appears to have started with a book published in 1922 called *Legends of Louisiana*, written by Helen Pitkin Schertz. The story originated from a chapter in the book titled "The Brother of the Sultan." There, Schertz wrote that a man arrived by ship in New Orleans, claiming to be the brother of the sultan of Turkey. According to Schertz, this story took place in 1792, when Louisiana was still technically under Spanish rule. The most obvious problem with Schertz's story is that it took place long before the Lepretre house had been built.

According to Schertz, when the sultan's ship first docked at New Orleans, the ship's captain negotiated with the harbormaster, asking that the locals provide a suitable home for someone as important and rich as the brother of a sultan. The harbormaster immediately realized that the only house in town that would meet the needs of so important a person was the home of Lepretre. Negotiations ensued and soon the sultan's brother was living in the home with his servants, eunuchs, and beautiful young "desert-girls." Some time passed, with the sultan's brother and his entourage amusing the locals with their strange customs and immense wealth. They kept to themselves and threw parties that could be heard on the streets by passersby, some of whom wandered by the house hoping to catch a glimpse of the mysterious tenants.

Then, one day, it all came to a bizarre end. No one stirred inside the house and deliverymen were unable to get answers at the door. After the better part of a day without getting anyone to answer at the door or any of the gates, someone decided it was necessary to force the door open. Inside, they found the sultan's brother with his throat slashed. At his feet were his five "child-women," likewise murdered. Authorities were summoned and someone decided to run down to the docks to see if anyone on the sultan's brother's ship might be able to provide some clues. The ship was gone. According to the story, the sultan's ship had been there the whole time but had now, overnight, simply vanished without notifying the harbormaster.

Schertz's story—and it is written in such a fashion that it can only be taken as fiction—then explains how various stories were floated to explain the bizarre events that took place in the Lepretre home. Also, the ship that had brought the sultan's brother had now become a pirate's ship, marauding on the high seas, while the Lepretre mansion was now haunted.

The Lepretre mansion would not be built until 1836. And there is no question that Schertz was describing the Lepretre mansion in her story. Her book contained only two stories, and the page before the chapter "The Sultan's Brother" contains a large photograph titled "The House of Tragic Mystery." It is a photo of the Lepretre mansion, and it is the only illustration in the entire book.

Some might wonder if it is possible that this story took place in a home on the same site, perhaps one that was displaced by the Lepretre mansion. This seems highly unlikely; the purchase price paid by Gardette for the lot would seem to be too small for the previous house on the site to be a mansion. And the property was owned by someone named Celestin Jung prior to July 25, 1836; Schertz does not mention this person.

Schertz's story also included Lepretre himself. How old would he have been if he had been present to negotiate with the sultan's brother in 1792? We know that Lepretre lost the house in a sheriff's sale in 1878. That means Lepretre was alive eighty-six years after Scherzer's story was said to have taken place. Unless Lepretre was no older than fourteen when he rented the house to the sultan's brother, he would have been over a hundred years old when he lost the home at the sheriff's auction.

Searches of old newspapers also do not reveal any murders taking place in the Lepretre mansion, nor any tales of a prince from a far-off land causing a commotion when he appeared at dockside with a heavily laden treasure ship and a bevy of harem "girls." It seems that the stories started, at least in print, with Schertz's book in 1922 and just grew from there.

Some of the tellings "corrected" the errors in her story and placed the events at the house during a time frame when the house existed. Many stories added details, of the sort more often found in ghost stories told around a campfire. *This Old House* repeated the myth that the murders were discovered when passersby saw blood flowing from under the front door, a fact that was not part of Schertz's version.

The National Park Service (NPS) began documenting historic buildings around the country in the 1930s, and the Historic American Buildings Survey (HABS) reports generated by the NPS are often a gold mine of information on old buildings. In 1958, a HABS report was created for the Lepretre mansion. Its author reviewed the long title history of the Lepretre mansion and noted the contract between Gardette and the builder. A long paragraph details the "amusing, but incredible story" of "The Brother of the Sultan," told by Schertz. It concludes, "As a result of the publication of this story, this house, which was unmistakably described, became known as LaPrete Mansion, and also as the House of the Turk." The HABS report places no credence in the story whatsoever.

In 1979, the *Times-Picayune* newspaper published an article titled "Life with an 'Exotic Ghost,'" which detailed the story of the sultan's brother and noted that much of the story made no sense and had no historical backing. "The story that has persisted down through the years . . ." "One fateful night, however, goes the story . . ." "Of course, as in the case of so many legends, there are some conflicting details . . ." The

Times-Picayune did not call the story a hoax, but it came close. It should have noted that as time went on, the stories became more detailed and fantastic. Some explained how the sultan had been found buried in the courtyard of the home, with all indications that he had been buried alive. Some even included stories of how the harem girls were all grossly dismembered and had all been raped before they were killed. None of the stories cite any primary sources—although they do often cite each other.

In 1966, a man named Anthony J. Vesick Jr. and an attorney named Frank J. D'Amico bought the house. For years, city buses had traveled past the home on Dauphine. In 1971, the city redrew its bus routes so that buses would drive by on Orleans and then turn onto Dauphine. Because of the nature of the roadway, which was narrow and not constructed for the thirty-three-thousand-pound buses, which is what they weighed when full, the house became subject to severe vibration. It was worse when the buses, more than five hundred a week, would sometimes cut across the street corner to avoid parked cars and hit the curb next to the house. Soon, the walls of the house showed signs of cracking.

Just as any self-respecting attorney would, D'Amico filed suit against the city for the damage to the home. After the court heard testimony regarding the condition of the home before and after the buses had been rerouted, the homeowners were awarded damages to repair the home.

While the murders were not real, the house is very real. It

contains nine bedrooms and ten bathrooms and comprises 7,057 square feet of living space. It is four stories tall and was listed for sale in 2013 with an asking price of $2.65 million. The seller suggested that the building could be turned into a six-apartment complex or restored back to its original form as a huge single-family home. The house is privately owned and is one of the most popular attractions on tours of New Orleans, particularly the ones focused on haunted houses and notorious crimes. It seems of little importance that no one was ever actually murdered in the house.

---

* Helen Pitkin Schertz, *Legends of Louisiana* (1922).
* Historic American Buildings Survey, *Le Pretre Mansion*, HABS No. 53.

Afterword

THE SALE OF A STIGMATIZED HOUSE

The number of murder homes that have changed hands in recent years raises the question: Is there an ethical or legal obligation for the seller of a murder house to disclose the true history of the home to prospective buyers? If a person was selling a home where someone had been brutally murdered, should they include that fact in the real-estate listing? If a person bought a murder house unknowingly, would they have legal grounds to file a lawsuit against the seller for not disclosing? Could they sue the real-estate agent?

As one might imagine, this sort of legal quandary has found its way into the U.S. court system several times, with interesting results. The most famous case in the field of "stigmatized" real estate is that of *Stambovsky v. Ackley*. In the late 1980s, Helen Ackley decided to sell her house in Nyack, New York. The house was beautiful, and according to an article she had written for *Reader's Digest*, it was also haunted. Ackley did not know the source of the poltergeists that she claimed occupied her house, but she was certain they were there. She also included her home in a "haunted house tour" of the city. When Jeffrey Stambovsky made an offer to buy the home, he claimed that he was not told of the ghosts.

After he had given Ackley a $32,500 down payment, he found out about the house's alleged haunting and sought to back out of the deal. Ackley refused. Stambovsky filed suit, hoping to get his money back. The first court to look at the suit simply threw it out. Who believes in ghosts? Stambovsky appealed, and a higher court ruled in his favor. Although the higher court did not weigh in on the existence or nonexistence of ghosts, the court noted that Ackley had written about, and advertised, the house as haunted—to everyone but Stambovsky. The court ruled that Ackley could not now say the house wasn't haunted in light of her previous statements about the property. The realness of the haunting was irrelevant: There was something very important about this house that she had believed to be true that she chose to not disclose to Stambovsky. Presumably, the same legal principle would apply to the sale of a murder house.

An earlier case with an actual murder house was even more on point, although not as famous. In California, Doris Reed bought a home from Robert King and found out from a neighbor that five people had been murdered in the house a decade before the sale. King had not mentioned this to Reed. To make matters worse, King had allegedly asked a neighbor to not tell Reed about the murders in the house. When she found out, Reed sought to unwind the sale. The first court that saw her lawsuit also threw it out. She appealed, and the California court that heard her appeal was more understanding. There were no allegations that the house was haunted. Here, it was simply the allegation that the murders had devalued the house. Reed argued that the house was worth less money because of its murderous history. Prospective buyers who knew the truth would not pay as much for the property. If she had known, she would not have paid as much for it either. She might not have even bought it. She had paid too much for it and if she were to sell, she would receive less for it as well. The appellate court sent the matter back to the trial court with instructions to let Reed pursue her claims, which, the court noted, were largely based on "pecuniary harm." That is, money. The court also pointed out how often it seemed to be the case that while sellers don't disclose the ugly history of the houses they sell, neighbors always seem willing to run over and spill the beans at the first sign of moving vans.

Interestingly, two university professors who study real-estate values at Wright State University became curious about the market for murder houses. As academics tend to do, James Larsen and Joseph Coleman came up with a label for them first: *psychologically impacted houses*. These were homes that had no physical defects but had been the site for an event that might cause a potential buyer to hesitate in closing a sale, such as a haunting, an illness, or a murder or suicide. The professors then gathered data on homes affected by these events and found out that they did, indeed, encounter problems in the marketplace. It wasn't catastrophic, but the homes did sell for 2.4 percent less than comparable homes. Worse, however, was that psychologically impacted houses took longer to sell. On average, these homes took 50 percent longer to find buyers.

While the 2.4 percent figure might not appear too significant, experts note that well-publicized murder houses, such as those in this book, often suffer larger drops in price. An appraiser named Randall Bell is considered to be an expert on helping with the pricing and sale of psychologically impacted houses. According to CNN, "Bell says a gruesome, well-publicized murder generally lowers a selling price by 15 to 35 percent." Of course, the "well-publicized" aspect of that equation means that it is less likely for a buyer to buy such a home without knowing it. It creates bigger problems for the seller, who must be willing to lower his or her price to find a buyer willing to overlook the home's past.

As you might imagine, some people are more than willing to help buyers and sellers of psychologically impacted houses. Besides the appraisers who help evaluate the homes, there are those who will help destigmatize the home. Since many murder houses are believed by some to be haunted, these experts will help rid the house of ghosts. There are also real-estate agents who specialize in selling psychologically impacted houses. One is Barry Lebow, who is based in Toronto. He even runs a popular seminar called "Selling the Haunted House:

Realtor Disclosure." He says his motto is: "Disclose unto others what you want disclosed unto you." In a nod to human nature, Lebow told CNN that a murder house in a small town might be a near-impossible sale. In that case he suggests, "Sell it to someone from the city."

Cases like this do not arise all that often, but when they do, they often make headlines. It was just a matter of time before people in the real-estate industry began wondering what might happen to them if they helped sell a home with a bad history and didn't disclose to the buyer. Might they be sued as well? Soon, laws were passed that protected real-estate salespeople and brokers who did not disclose that a particular property was stigmatized. The laws varied wildly from state to state—more than half of the United States have these laws now—and some do not address the murder house scenario at all but instead focus on other things a seller might not disclose. For instance, a seller in Nevada might find legal problems down the road for not disclosing that the house being sold had been used previously as a meth lab.

Some states do require disclosure of a murder house's status, but only under limited circumstances. In California, a seller only needs to inform a buyer of a death that has occurred on the property in the three years preceding the sale. In other words, the "murder house" disclosure requirement expires three years after the murders. And, just to make these cases more confusing, some states protect brokers and real-estate agents who do not disclose, but leave the actual seller open to lawsuits. How would a buyer guarantee they are not buying a murder house? Ask the seller and ask the agent. If all else fails, ask the next-door neighbors. They seem to be the ones who know and always seem willing to disclose all the gory details.

---

* Les Christie, "House Haunting We Will Go," CNNMoney.com, October 28, 2003.

* Brendan Kennedy, "Buyer Unaware of Orangeville Home's History, Abandons Sale," *Toronto Star*, September 30, 2011.

ACKNOWLEDGMENTS

I'll be the first to admit that this is an unusual book. I have no idea what fascinates people about murders or murder houses or what draws them to go look at them, but there is no denying that the fascination appears to be almost universal. The book was fun to write in that regard—I find these stories interesting too—but it required a lot of legwork. In that sense, it was different from anything I have worked on previously. Each chapter, each house, required a whole new avenue of research. There was almost no overlap among the stories, so I had to start from scratch on each chapter. Some of these were quite easy to find information on, while others were more difficult. Entire books have been written on several of these murders, but I was limited by space considerations. For these I tried to summarize, and include the most important and interesting facts.

One minor note I feel I must include here: On the few occasions where a murderer has never been conclusively identified, as in Villisca, I use the masculine pronoun to describe the killer. While modern writing often eschews the use of gender-specific pronouns when a person's identity is truly unknown, it is quite well known that most psychopathic killers, especially mass and serial murderers, are male. In this case, I am merely playing the odds.

For those interested in the legal aspects of the murders described here, I highly recommend the Famous Trials website built by Douglas O. Linder from the University of Missouri–Kansas City School of Law. Only four of the murders in this book are featured on the site, but the amount of information he has assembled is remarkable. Ever wonder about the trials of Galileo, the Salem Witches, Al Capone, or Patty Hearst? The site contains write-ups of more than six dozen famous trials through history, including photographs and excerpts of transcripts. More are being added all the time. See http://law2.umkc.edu/faculty/projects/ftrials/ftrials.htm. Or simply search on the phrase "famous trials" and you will find it.

I could not have written this book without immense help I received from generous friends, ones I met while working on this book and others I have known for many years. Lee Ann Wilber at the Lizzie Borden Bed & Breakfast Museum spent time with me on the phone and gave me many details I could only learn from someone who spent time in the house on a daily basis. Sean Coxen shared information and photos of the Rehmeyer "Hex" House in Pennsylvania. It is one thing to see photos of the house; it is another to speak to the person who took the photos and hear their impressions, the things that cameras cannot record.

J. Ross McGinnis extended me the professional courtesy, attorney-to-attorney, of speaking to me on the phone about the

Rehmeyer murder trials. His knowledge of the crimes and the aftermath is encyclopedic, and he did a wonderful job of helping me understand it well enough to where I could put it down in plain English. I also received an amazing amount of help from people like Caitlin Foyt, a woman who just happened to have taken photos of the LaBianca house that she kindly let me use.

And, as I have often done before, I must thank Thomas Spademan, one of my oldest friends. He and I are the same age so he is not the "oldest" in that sense; it is just that we have been friends for so long. Tom is a professor and philosopher but has a knack for genealogical research, which translates quite well into finding out things about people who lived a long time ago. Some of the more recent murder houses were easy to find information on, but some of the earlier ones seemed to have left little or no historical trail. In those cases, I often found myself consulting Tom and asking him if he could track down some information for me. Often, it was about the victims, or the survivors, or the descendants of the people in these stories. Regardless, he always got me more information that I expected, faster than I thought possible.

I must also thank my agent, Steve Harris; my editor, Danielle Stockley; and Meredith Giordan, who first had the idea that a book like this should be written.

John Ferracane must be thanked as well. He is the friend in the first paragraph of this book who had lunch with me in Miami Beach at the News Café, where Gianni Versace bought his magazines the day Cunanan senselessly shot him to death. I had been talking to John about how there was one murder house in Miami

Beach where he lived at the time, and I mentioned the News Café. John was familiar with it and suggested we eat lunch there and walk down and see the Versace mansion afterward. The mansion, the café, the hotel where Cunanan was staying, and the houseboat where he hid were all in the general vicinity of where John lived at the time, and he helped me map all of them out.

And I must thank my friends, many of whom mentioned names of potential subjects for me when I told them I was working on this book. Active and lively discussions are the only way to make sure a book is assembled properly. Of course I thank my wife, Jennifer, who is a true-crime buff as well, who heard me tell and retell many of these stories as I fleshed them out. Thank you.

Finally, I must thank Brandy and Sangria for protecting the house from intruders, real and imaginary. And of course, Milo and Wolfy, who keep me company as I write. Without them, my work would be impossible.

ABOUT THE AUTHOR

Steve Lehto is an author and attorney from southeast Michigan. He was also an adjunct professor of both law and history at the University of Detroit–Mercy. Among his previous books are *The Great American Jet Pack: The Quest for the Ultimate Individual Lift Device* (2013), *Death's Door: The Truth Behind the Italian Hall Disaster and the Strike of 1913* (2013), *Drawn to Injustice: The Wrongful Conviction of Timothy Masters* (2012), *Chrysler's Turbine Car: The Rise and Fall of Detroit's Coolest Creation* (2010), and *Michigan's Columbus: The Life of Douglass Houghton* (2009). He has written for magazines such as *Lake Superior, Mopar Action, Michigan History,* and the *Michigan Bar Journal.* His work has appeared on the websites *Jalopnik* and the *Huffington Post.* He has been interviewed on CNN, the BBC, *Good Morning America,* and countless other radio and television outlets. He is a frequent speaker and has appeared in several documentaries as well. Follow him on Twitter: @stevelehto.